Crossings ON THE FERRIES OF PUGET SOUND
by Michael Diehl

Crossings is available in both soft-cover and hard-bound formats. To obtain a copy of *Crossings* in a format other than this one, contact a bookseller, the publisher or **CrossingsOnPugetSound.com**.

ISBN-13: 978-0-9818815-0-8 [hard cover]
ISBN-10: 0-9818815-0-5

ISBN-13: 978-0-9818815-1-5 [soft cover]
ISBN-10: 0-9818815-1-3

Library of Congress system cataloging data is available at CrossingsOnPugetSound.com.

Crossings includes five graphic images that were created for the Washington State Ferries ("WSF") system. WSF authorized the reproduction in this book of two scanned images from the WSF's "Sailing Schedule" – its cover, with a Puget Sound route map, and a timetable for one route – as well as an image from the system's website (another map) and two sketches of WSF ferries.

Printed in South Korea — First Printing (August 2008)

Published by –

Island Earth Publications
P.O. Box 10218
Bainbridge Island, Washington
98110-0218

Crossings resulted from the kind encouragement of many people who responded to an Internet posting of ferry-related photographs and writing with evident pleasure – in particular ferry crew member Emmanuelle Donaldson, Chief Petty Officer, United States Navy (Retired). Without the support and great patience of Judith, however, suggestions that the posting become a book would have remained only an idea.

Crossings

ON THE FERRIES
OF PUGET SOUND

Michael Diehl

This is an essay about ferries
and the patterns of their passages
in the ephemeral light on Puget Sound;
seas, shores and mountains meeting sky;
human handiwork and Earth's enduring elements;
and what may be found on a crossing of these waters.

Introduction: Puget Sound greets a voyaging ferry with panoramic vistas, expansive stretches of water, and a vast overarching sky. Everything visible from aboard the boat is continuously transformed during the voyage.

The water, sky and landscapes around the Sound respond to the characteristics of the season, the time of day, the particular weather of the moment, and the position of the Sun. When a ferry alters course, the world seems to rotate ponderously around it. Actual breezes mix with the apparent wind created by the vessel's motion. The steel decks vibrate underfoot. Distant muted mechanical rumblings provide a deep undertone accompanying the higher-pitched hiss of water spraying aside and foaming as its elastic surface is sliced open by the ferry's hull.

For those new to the experience of a crossing, unconcealed wonder and delight are normal and visible reactions.

Thousands living in northwestern Washington ride the ferries daily; many others do so only occasionally. The Seattle area also hosts an estimated 9 million visitors each year. Many of them who have studied guidebooks or received sage advice from local contacts take time for an outing aboard a ferry traveling on Puget Sound, to enjoy a signature Seattle experience.

First-time and occasional ferry riders enter an unfamiliar world – an unusual mass transit system that journeys across water and that could easily be mistaken for a scenic cruise service. The passengers who sustain this mass transit system, however, are commuters, predominantly people who voyage into Seattle each weekday for work and at the end of the day travel back across the Sound once more to return to their homes.

Many commuters cross the Sound 500 times a year, and so may well believe they have seen it all before. First-time passengers have not, and so ask questions: "Where is Mount Rainier?"; "Who rides these boats?"; "How many people does this ferry carry?"; "How deep is Puget Sound?"; or "What is that mountain?"

Crossings depicts what can be seen on Puget Sound and answers such questions.

A key truth about traveling on the Sound is that all transits are different, some dramatically so and others far more subtly.

The only day-to-day constant for a sailing at 4:40 p.m. or any other scheduled time is the position of the hands on a clock. The Sun's place in the sky is no longer precisely where it was at that time the day before, and will be different once more the day after. The exact route the ferry takes will vary – ferries do not travel on railroad tracks, and vessels may shape their courses because of the wind, other ship traffic, and the presence or absence of tidal flows. The surface waters of the Sound can be calm or whipped by a storm, blue or gray, tinged with green by spring blooms of aquatic life, or stained like tea by autumn storm runoff from tannin-rich plant debris swept into

Seen from aboard a westbound ferry, a sailboat headed to Seattle passes close alongside as the day's last light brushes across Mount Rainier.

the Sound from its shores. The surface textures of the water respond to winds, tidal currents, and the past passages of other ships. The time of year, time of day, and clouds and weather of the moment reshape the surroundings for each voyage.

Mount Rainier may be powerfully present or wholly hidden, and the Cascades and Olympics Ranges can be invisible behind haze or clouds, or starkly evident to the east and west.

Natural factors create this variability – the influences of the surrounding mountain ranges; seasonal changes; weather patterns; and the particular characteristics of northwestern light. Such forces are interwoven with what will be experienced on any transit of the Sound, and the voyage may be enhanced for a ferry passenger who considers them.

Daily transits in all seasons offer commuters the opportunity to witness the many moods of the Sound. Those who peruse these pages may enter their world, travel with them, and partake of what any ferry passenger may see.

Sections and themes –
momentary reflections ...

**A few facts,
for those who do not already know them:**

In *Crossings*, text boxes like this one provide information of a factual nature. Details are presented about subjects such as the ferries, how the transit system functions, the Sound, and the surrounding areas.

This factual material may be of particular interest to those who are visiting or curious about a specific topic, or of a continually questioning nature.

Sections and pages that focus predominantly on such factual information are distinguished by the use of a light gray page background.

Reflections on routes across the Sound

Puget Sound divides the densely populated Seattle area on its eastern shore from two peninsulas to the west. The Olympic Peninsula is the westernmost part of Washington State and the larger of these two westside land masses. Its western face looks out onto the Pacific, and its northern side faces Canada's Vancouver Island, across the Strait of Juan de Fuca. The long "L" of the Hood Canal runs from north to south along the eastern shore of the Olympic Peninsula and also delineates the western shorelines of the Kitsap Peninsula. On Kitsap's eastern face, Puget Sound separates the Kitsap Peninsula from the rest of the State, including the Sound's eastern side and Seattle.

Ferries link these bodies of land, providing more direct access than is offered by roads that curve around the edges of the Sound's many arms.

Five main routes operate in the Seattle metropolitan area, with regular service each day, transporting vehicles and people each way. From north to south, these routes link Mukilteo, north of Seattle, to Clinton on Whidbey Island; Edmonds, also north of Seattle, with Kingston near the northern end of the Kitsap Peninsula; central Seattle with Bainbridge Island (connected to Kitsap by a bridge); central Seattle and Bremerton; and through a three-legged route, Fauntleroy in south Seattle, Vashon Island, and Kitsap County's Southworth.

Other routes offer access to Islands – in the north, from Anacortes to the San Juans and from Port Townsend, on the Olympic Peninsula, to Keystone on Whidbey. To the south, a short route connects Tacoma and Vashon Island.

Images in *Crossings* are primarily from the Seattle/Bainbridge Island route, but are similar to what can be seen during any ferry passage on the Sound.

A crossing can be measured in many ways. On a ferry, a passage between the Seattle and Bainbridge Island terminals traverses just under nine miles in about 35 minutes. For a seagull, the direct line of travel is indifferent to the shoal waters ferries must avoid, and so the gull's flight between those points can be shorter by almost a full mile. For passengers aboard a ferry, the journey might be measured by what they experience during a transit, or by the contrasts between the two end-points of their journey.

True skyscrapers are visible from the Sound – parallel mountain ranges, with the line of the Cascades jutting skyward east of Seattle and, west of the Kitsap Peninsula, the peaks of the Olympics marching north.

Those mountains frame the Sound, form its weather, and can fill the horizon. At times they are crisply visible from the ferries, but often are hidden and shrouded by clouds.

On the Sound's eastern and western shores, the spaces between the mountains and water are distinctly different. The Kitsap Peninsula shorelines are still largely cloaked with trees, facing from afar the serried line of sharp-edged forms of the office buildings that stand on the hills across the Sound.

Facing page: The outer Cascades behind south downtown Seattle.

Above: A Bainbridge Island shoreline and Mount Constance.

23

Outside of the summer tourist season, it is the thousands of commuters who live in Kitsap County but work in the Seattle metro area who constitute the majority of ferry traffic.

The busiest weekday sailings are those leaving the westside between 6:00 and 9:00 a.m., and afternoon return trips between 3:30 and 6:20 p.m., but ferries start running from the Kitsap side of the Sound as early as 4:45 a.m.

For those commuters from the westside, a year presents a cycle – winter means pre-dawn departures and after-dark homecomings; in fall and spring, the Sun may rise and set during their two daily passages; during the summer, the long northwestern days illuminate both transits of the Sound.

Changing seasons are part of what alters each crossing.

Counterclockwise, from facing page:

Before dawn, a ferry stands ready to take on embarking passengers at Bainbridge Island; the last cars enter the ferry's "car tunnel"; the final wave of bicycle commuters boards; and foot passengers stream down an elevated ramp and across a gangway onto the ferry.

Except in summer, almost all early morning commuters move directly inside after they board, seeking the comforts of the ferry's enclosed main deck – booths, soft seats, a galley, and climate control. Few venture up one level to the open "sun deck". Those who do so, and who then walk to the Seattle end of the ferry while it is loading, can greet dawn breaking over the Sound and the entrance to Eagle Harbor, and a canvas of sea and sky that rarely repeats its display exactly from one day to another.

On different days dawn paints with washes of violet, gradations of gray and orange, red, or black, or shades of deep sea-blue. The surface of the Sound, the sky, and light create a new tapestry of textures and colors each morning.

The Sun's first light may reveal transient fog above the surface of the Sound, or randomly highlight clouds and a shining streak of slick water on the sea's surface.

As the ferry churns out of its slip on Bainbridge Island and moves east, towards the mouth of Eagle Harbor, the panorama opens. To the south, Mount Rainier may glide out from behind the silhouetted conifers that have concealed it from sight and, eight miles across the Sound to the east, Seattle's full skyline will emerge from concealment behind Wing Point.

While the ferry travels, the Earth is spinning with it. The Sun climbs higher into the sky, and the early-day light flooding onto the Sound changes.

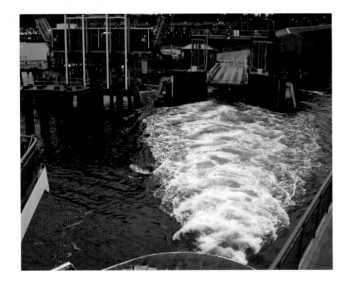

The straight-line route from Eagle Harbor eastward to Seattle is blocked, for ferries, by a gravelly spit running southeast from Wing Point, at the harbor's mouth. To avoid it, ferries turn south and will steer for a mile almost directly towards Mount Rainier.

Sightings of that mountain are never guaranteed. It is entirely invisible one day, capped by clouds on another, and at times presents only a distant misty cone rising from a layer of haze floating over the patterned surfaces of the Sound.

On this southerly leg out of Eagle Harbor, one side of the ferry faces the morning Sun, as the other side looks away.

While the ferry leaving Bainbridge is traveling south along that Island's shore, its sister ship is leaving Seattle behind on its own westward passage towards Bainbridge Island.

After the Seattle-bound boat turns east, the two ferries will cross in mid-Sound, keeping to a rhythm of near-simultaneous transits that shuttle continually between the two terminals.

Facing page: The Tacoma *moves away from downtown Seattle as she begins a voyage towards Bainbridge Island.*

Below: The ferry sailing from Bainbridge Island leaves a curved wake as it makes the "big turn" to the east after traveling about a mile south along the Island's shore.

Two ferries shown here are both headed west in mid-Sound, as seen from an eastbound ferry on its way from Bainbridge Island to Seattle.

The Tacoma, in the foreground, is going to Bainbridge; the Kitsap, behind her, is bound for Bremerton.

A distant third ferry, traveling between Southworth and Vashon Island but barely visible through the morning haze, can be seen at the far left.

As the ferry nears Seattle, it enters Elliott Bay, a large sheltered harbor notched into the eastern shore of the Sound. Passengers begin to move forward, to claim a spot on the bow. The regulars who venture there every day may see, on some mornings, Elliott Bay dappled with light, or ...

... the angular blocks of unaltered
buildings under ever-changing skies.

For those gathering on the decks outside, the nearing city speaks to other senses. The sound of traffic arrives first, usually well offshore when the ferry's engines slow to allow gliding into the slip, but sometimes even earlier, on windstill days. At first, the road sound is a quiet steady roar of white noise, like a distant mountain stream, but without the natural variations that make such sounds so soothing.

As the ferry moves closer to the city, the roadway roar escalates until it overpowers the sound of the wind. And when there is a northeasterly breeze, a thick odor can spread from the city far out onto the bay – hot cooking oils, the scents of thousands of morning meals, mingled with the fumes of countless cars, sometimes spiced by the faint sharp aroma of coffee.

As the ferry draws closer to the Pier 52 ferry terminal, the city's bustling presence becomes overwhelmingly pervasive.

Elliott Bay is a busy working harbor and ocean port. Ferries entering the Bay pass ships at anchor and tugs towing barges or guiding freighters into or out of docks. There is a bulk cargo terminal along the northeastern shore, and a sprawling containerized cargo shipping terminal and drydock facilities are located on and around Harbor Island in the southern reaches of Elliott Bay.

Facing page: Mount Rainier stands behind the cranes of the containerized cargo facilities that line the shores on and around Harbor Island.

Built in the watercourse of the Duwamish River and completed in 1909, Harbor Island's 350 acres made it the largest man-made island in the world until 1938, when a larger project surpassed it (Treasure Island, constructed in the San Francisco Bay).

Harbor Island has since been expanded to 407 acres, and remains the world's second largest man-made island.

Passengers standing on the ferry's foredeck have a front row position for watching vessel traffic.

As the ferry approaches the shore, a crowd builds on the foredeck. The first to move outside will stand just inboard of the deck's yellow "stay back" line, even on ferries where that line no longer exists. The area behind them soon fills and, inside on the main deck, people cluster near the doors. There are buses to catch, offices to open, appointments to keep, or, for some, perhaps, just a daily game or exercise routine. As the ferry docks, the passengers wait for the rattling removal of the gangway chains and the fall of the safety net.

The leaders of the exodus might be called the "Seattle Sprinters" – once they have been released, they are ready to advance swiftly through the terminal's passageways onto divergent routes that lead off into the far reaches of the city.

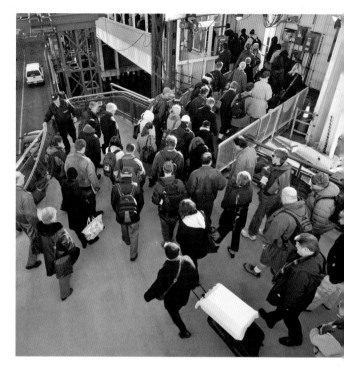

Bursts of the dock-end propeller slow the boat, so that it can move gently shoreward between two "wingwalls" (upright angled guides for the ferry's bow). Once the ferry has come to rest with its nose under the raised vehicle ramp, that ramp is lowered. Bicyclists are usually the first off, even before the foot-passenger gangway has been hoisted into place on the deck above and secured. Only then can the walk-ons disembark.

The first rush of people offloading is followed by a slower, steady flow. Most of those disembarking will move among the central mass of passengers. Some, working with a more leisurely plan and pace, will linger on the ferry until the main crowd has entirely dissipated, and only then make their less hurried way into the city from the nearly empty boat.

The Seattle ferry terminal on Pier 52 is a hub for the system. It serves the two car ferry routes for Bremerton and Bainbridge Island, as well as a "fast foot ferry" that runs to Vashon Island. Ferries can arrive or depart in tandem when their route rhythms coincide.

Even during the peak travel hours (barring delays from cars that fail to start and other problems), crews typically offload and reload a ferry in about 15 minutes. As vehicles drive away and foot passengers head into the city, outbound vehicles and travelers accumulate in the terminal area, waiting to board.

Facing page: Foot passengers head into a tunnel under the Alaskan Way viaduct and eastward into downtown Seattle as the last vehicles are offloaded.

Below: Ferries leave for Bremerton and Vashon Island while the Bainbridge Island ferry unloads.

The ferry is emptied of all cars and people. A security sweep causes a brief pause. Then boarding begins anew, with bicyclists first. As they pedal into the car tunnel, the walk-on passengers move along an elevated walkway that leads to the main deck above the vehicle tunnel.

Once the first wave of bicyclists has loaded, the motorcycles then roar aboard. All larger vehicles follow, with ambulances and car pools given priority in loading.

Trucks are directed into the center "car tunnel", where the high overhead provides ample clearance for trailers and other tall loads. Cars are distributed both in the tunnel and along two tiers with lower ceilings along the ferry's outboard sides.

As ferries load and sail from one terminal, an inexact mirror image of those activities is taking place across the Sound at the sister terminal. Departures from the two terminals for each route are scheduled to be nearly simultaneous, establishing a regular rhythm of sailings that continues throughout the day.

Facing page: Two ferries head west from Seattle on their early morning rounds. The closer one, the Tillikum, *is bound for Bremerton, and the* Tacoma, *more distant, is headed to Bainbridge.*

At left: A ferry leaves Bainbridge Island's Eagle Harbor, heading east, its scheduled departure timed to synchronize with the sailing from Seattle of a ferry making a voyage to the Island.

Facts about ferries and the ferry system:

The Ferry System: Until the early 1900s, ferry service on Puget Sound was provided by unregulated private carriers, known collectively as the "Mosquito Fleet". Service gradually consolidated under two companies – the Puget Sound Navigation Company (operating as the "Black Ball" line) and the Kitsap County Transportation Company. After the Kitsap line failed, the Black Ball line was the dominant provider of ferry service until 1951, when the State of Washington bought most of that company's boats and took over the transportation function as the Washington State Ferries ("WSF") system, a division of the State's Department of Transportation.

WSF operates 10 routes and 20 terminals, with about 450 sailings daily. Each year, the WSF system handles some 24 million passenger transits, roughly half for commuters, and uses about 17 million gallons of fuel.

During most of 2007, WSF's fleet included 28 ferries, and 27 were in service that year. The fleet's three largest boats are in the "Jumbo Mark II Class" – the *Tacoma*, *Wenatchee*, and *Puyallup* – each rated to carry 2,500 passengers and more than 200 cars. Two of these typically are in use each day for Seattle/Bainbridge Island service, the system's most heavily traveled route.

These "Jumbo Mark II Class" vessels were built in Seattle in the late 1990s, use diesel-electric (AC) engines rated as having 13,200 horsepower, and can cruise at 18 knots. These boats are 460'2" long, and have a beam-width of 90' and a 17'3" draft. The two smallest ferries in the WSF fleet are the 250-passenger, 25-knot *Skagit* and *Kalema* (fast "foot ferries" that do not carry vehicles).

Most Central Sound car ferry routes are served by slightly smaller boats in various design and size classes – the "Jumbo Class", "Super Class", "Issaquah Class" and "Evergreen State Class" boats. In November 2007, deterioration was found in the hulls of some of WSF's four 80-year-old "Steel Electric Class" ferries (most of the WSF fleet's smaller car ferries), and those boats were removed from active service.

One WSF route (between Keystone and Port Townsend) requires a smaller boat with shallow draft. Otherwise, specific boats are not permanently dedicated to any particular route. When a ferry is "down" for maintenance so that a route needs a substitute boat, WSF shuffles its fleet to cover the route.

A vehicle transport ferry defines itself according to its direction of travel. And that changes for each crossing. "Drive-on/drive-off" ferries thus have no fixed "bow" or "stern" (or permanent "fore" and "aft") – instead, each has an "No. 1 End" and a "No. 2 End". For efficiency, so that the ferries never waste time turning around, and to allow vehicles to drive forward both while loading and while unloading, the ferries have propellers, rudders, and drive-on/drive-off vehicle entrances at each end.

In docking, side-to-side movements are accomplished by using combinations of the rudders and propellers located at the boat's opposite ends to maneuver the ferry.

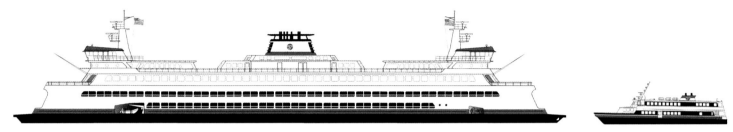

The 460-foot Tacoma *(at left) and the 112-foot* Skagit *(at right), in approximate relative scale.*

Engine power also is used during offloading and loading to stabilize the ferry in its slip, instead of multiple heavy mooring lines that would take time to attach and detach. Where the ferry's nose meets the car ramp, two angled rows of upright pilings forming "wingwalls" provide a notch for the shore-end "bow" of the boat. While the ferry is in its slip, the propeller at the "aft" end is running just fast enough to keep the ferry nudged up against the wingwalls. Alongside, one or more other large stationary fender structures (called "dolphins") – either moored or sunk into the bottom – provide a surface against which the side of the ferry can be stabilized by angling the aft rudder as the propeller turns. At departure, a ferry can leave without prolonged line-handling delays.

In the slip, lines are used at two locations: Heavy "head lines" are run from ashore to cleats on the vehicle deck, and lighter tethers fasten the gangway to the railing on the main passenger deck. These lines stabilize those two loading points but can be quickly placed and removed.

Service between Seattle and Bainbridge Island:
The route between Seattle and Bainbridge Island, the busiest one in the WSF system, is served by the fleet's largest car ferries – those in the "Jumbo Mark II Class".

According to WSF data for 2007, the ferries providing transits between Seattle and Bainbridge hauled nearly 2.1 million vehicles (each with a driver), including about 800,000 commercial vehicles, and handled a total of 6.4 million transit "riders" (vehicles with drivers, cyclists, passengers riding in vehicles, and foot passengers). Within the foot-passenger category (3 million transits each year), a large percentage consists of commuters who work in Seattle but live on the Kitsap Peninsula or even farther west – each commuter ordinarily accounts for two trips a day. With 6.4 million passenger transits a year on this route, the daily average (at about 17,500 people) is almost exactly seven "boat loads" for the largest WSF ferries, with their capacities of 2,500 passengers.

Reflections on Puget Sound

The Sound is bounded on the east and west by two ranges of mountains, and was formed by them. Glaciers flowing south were channeled between those barriers, excavating as they moved. As the glaciers retreated and their melting ice replenished the oceans, rising waters filled the Sound.

The Sound reflects events that happened millions of years ago, when the mountains rose, and tens of thousands of years ago, when the last rivers of ice retreated north.

The mountains still shape the Sound.

Facing page: The Tacoma, *sailing eastward from Bainbridge Island, leaves the Olympics behind.*

From the Bainbridge end of a ferry leaving the Island's terminal, the mountains begin to appear over the Island on the horizon to the west. As the ferry travels farther east out onto the Sound, a ferry left behind at the terminal (the Illahee*) shrinks as the Olympics gradually reveal their full height.*

The mountain ranges paralleling the Sound affect the region's weather. The Pacific is an immense "heat sink" whose temperature alters only marginally as the seasons change. That reservoir of near-constant temperature moderates the local climate, providing cooling during the summer and warmth in winter. The currents of the Northern Pacific Gyre mimic the Gulf Stream, acting as powerful hydraulic conveyer of equatorial heat into northern Pacific waters.

During winter months, air passing above the ocean's surface off the Washington coast collects warmth and moisture. The region's predominant southwesterly winds sweep in from the sea, carrying that saturated air onto the western shores of the State. South of the Olympics, the moist blanket moves inland and, when inland temperatures are colder than the air over the ocean, the cooling of the humid air produces steady rains in a zone extending far inland.

The peaks of the Olympics, however, force incoming moist air upwards, into much colder regions, where the air's ability to retain moisture is reduced. The winter rains along the west coast of the Peninsula are prodigious, but not like the brief torrential downpours of southern and desert states. Instead, the west-face rain at times is almost constant, hour after hour, day after day, week after week. Some of the temperate rainforests on the Olympic Peninsula's western slope receive as much as 200 inches of rain each year.

East and northeast of the Olympics, incoming southwesterly fronts sink down into the basin of the Sound, but they have been wrung out. Rain falls, and the skies are gray, but the area experiences mist, drizzle and showers far more often than heavy storms (although those, too, come at times, from fronts that have avoided the Olympics and twisted their way into the basin from the north or south).

As storm fronts move to the east, the Cascades Range repeats the drying process, squeezing residual moisture out of air forced upwards into the cold once again. Beyond the Cascades to the east, the State becomes relatively arid.

The region around the Sound has many micro-climates. Forests on the Olympics' western face are rain-soaked gardens of trees and moss. On the inland side of the Olympics, there is a "rain shadow" where the desiccated clouds passing by overhead seldom leave heavy rain below. (Sequim, a town on the northern face of the Olympic Peninsula, boasts having an average rainfall each year of less than 20 inches.)

The Sun breaks through black clouds at dawn over Seattle.

Facing page: Layered clouds near sunrise create dances of light on the surface of the Sound's waters.

Far right: Mid-winter sunset from a ferry sailing out of Seattle towards the Olympics.

The topography diverts storms into complex paths and creates convergence zones, where the winds from fronts that were split by the mountains blow into the Sound from the south and north and collide again west of the Cascades.

The skies embody these conditions – clouds at times lie like a thick gray featherbed over the area, but winds can and do tear openings where blue skies and sunshine can be seen.

More often, the cloud cover presents as rows of parallel clouds, or several layers at different heights. In the spaces between rows of clouds or the gaps and holes among them, rays of light will gleam through onto the Sound for moments or hours ("sun-breaks"), sometimes almost as if a spotlight had been turned on to highlight a chosen feature of the Earth, and at other times as if a theatrical lighting designer had been given free rein to create a light show on all of the area's mountains, islands, waters, and the ever-varying formations of clouds.

Summer is different. The sunny days of July through September typically are repetitive, with many days just like the ones before and after. Likewise, the winter months bring some periods of incessant slate-gray skies, but even then, and far more so in the spring and fall, the area realizes its potential for moments or hours of fast-changing displays of light, shadow and color.

Except at the height of summer, the Sun lies relatively low on the horizon. As everywhere in latitudes closer to the poles than 40 degrees north or south, the Sun never is directly overhead, and its light is slanting and somehow softer than in lands closer to the Equator, and clouds seem far more varied. These are high-latitude skies.

Facts about how the region was formed:

The Shape of the Sound: Puget Sound lies in a lowlands trough between two ranges of mountains – the Olympics to the west and the Cascades to the east. Measured north to south from Oak Harbor on Whidbey Island to Olympia, Washington's capital city, the basin of the Sound spans approximately 86 miles. At Seattle's latitude, measured from east to west, the lowlands area between the two mountain ranges is about 50 miles wide.

The boundaries along the east and west sides of the trough are defined by those two jagged lines of craggy mountains, cupping the Sound between their heights. The basin of the Sound ends on the north where the Strait of Juan de Fuca cuts across the top of the Olympic Peninsula. To the south, the land flattens at the foot of that peninsula, where the mountains end and rolling hills span the miles between Olympia and the Pacific Ocean to the west and Oregon to the south.

Formation of the Region: The coastline of the west and northwestern United States parallels a subduction zone – a wandering but primarily north-south line where one tectonic plate (the Continental Plate) is continuously moving to the west against and then over the resistance of plates underneath the Pacific Ocean.

The topography of the region was formed during millions of years by the ongoing, almost imperceptibly gradual collision of multiple tectonic plates.

The Cascades, estimated to be as old as 50 million years, were created by terranes (small pieces of tectonic plate, often evidenced by an arc of upthrust islands) that "docked" against the land (or crashed, there, in the slow way that tectonic plates do that). Parts of the terranes were scraped off as the ocean-floor plate was ground under the continent. The mass and force of the collision caused upward buckling on the leading edge of the Continental Plate, gradually forming mountains.

The Olympics rose about 24 million years ago, as a new terrane "docked" against the Cascades terrane and about 50 other terranes that already had lodged against the growing continent before the arrival of the plates that drove up the peaks of Olympics.

The forces at play beneath the Earth's surface have not worked alone in shaping the Sound. As mountains rose, they were challenged by wind, rain, and ice.

For a prolonged period ending some 15,000 years ago, the Sound lay under the most recent of the many cyclical visits of glaciers that have poured slowly down the Puget Sound trough from Canada.

Flowing south from British Columbia, the "Cordilleran" ice sheets began in the coastal mountains of that region, merged with other alpine glaciers and then ran south to the northern shoulders of the Olympics, where they split, part of the flow gouging its way west to the Pacific and the other scooping out the deep grooves that became Puget Sound and the Hood Canal.

The most recent glacial advance (the Vashon Strade of the Fraser Glaciation) spread a blanket of ice about 6,000 feet thick at the present U.S./Canada border and 3,000 feet deep over the site of modern-day Seattle.

Ice filled the Puget Sound basin, stretching from the mountains located on its eastern side to the Olympics on the west. In geologic time, or the lifetime of the Cascades, that most recent glaciation ended only very recently – a mere one one-thousandth of the time those mountains are thought to have existed, the equivalent of just two weeks in the past for a 50-year-old human.

The outer mountains of the Olympics and Cascades ranges were just tall enough to constrain the flow of ice. The height of Big Snow Mountain, about 40 miles east of Seattle, is typical of the outer western Cascades peaks. It stands 6,670 feet tall. Taller peaks farther east, in the inner Cascades roughly 60 miles from Seattle, approach 9,000 feet in height.

Across the Sound, on the Olympic Peninsula and 36 miles west of Seattle, the twin peaks of The Brothers stand 6,866 feet above sea level. The inner peaks of the Olympics Range rise to 7,000 to 8,000 feet.

A line drawn from Big Snow Mountain to the Brothers covers about 70 miles, passes through Seattle and crosses Bainbridge Island. On a ferry in the middle of a crossing, on a brilliantly clear winter day, a passenger can look east and then west, seeing walls of mountains behind both Seattle and the Island, roughly equidistant, roughly alike in height, ruggedly towering above the Sound and the buildings and trees that line it.

To the northeast and southeast in dramatic isolation stand two pyramids, the volcanic cones of Mount Baker and Mount Rainier, both far younger than the two predominant mountain ranges, and bubbled into existence much more recently by upwellings from the deep crushing pressures of tectonic plates.

Above: The outer, lower fringes of the Cascades rear up behind north central Seattle and the Space Needle.

At right: Mount Baker, 90 miles north-northeast of Seattle and 10,775 feet in height, is only occasionally visible from ferries on the Bainbridge route.

Below: The eastern face of the Olympics, as seen from a ferry offshore of Seattle. Eagle Harbor is marked by the buildings along the shoreline directly behind the sailboat.

Major peaks in this view of the Olympics Range are, from south (left) to north (right):

The Brothers

Mt. Anderson

Mt. Jupiter

Mt. Constance

Warrior Peaks

At left: Mount Rainier, 14,411 feet tall and about 68 miles south-southeast of Seattle, stands apart from and far taller than the line of the Cascades.

79

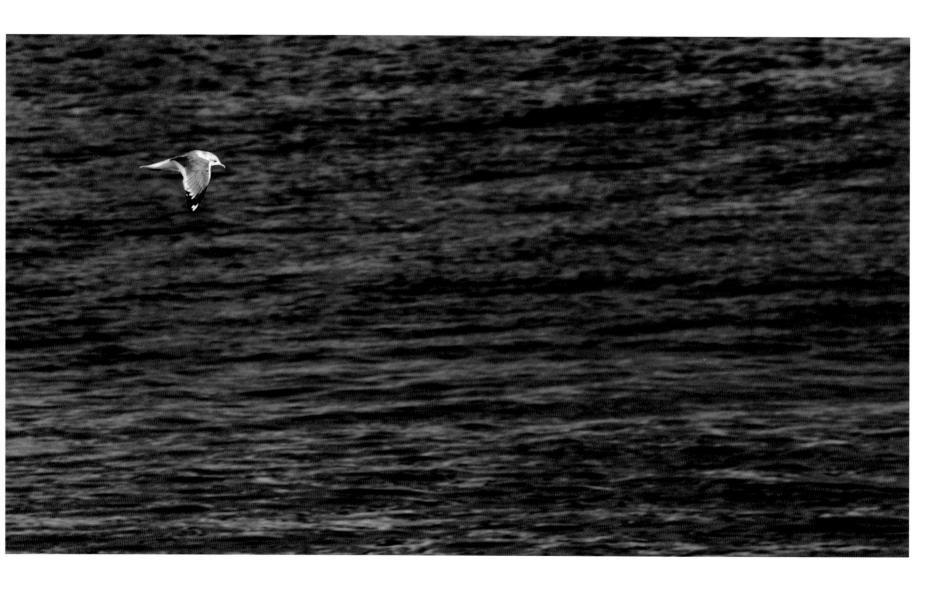

Reflections on hard edges and soft forms

The Washington ferries are quintessential human artifacts. The area through which they travel, if it is viewed from a sufficient distance, remains predominantly natural.

A ferry passage brings steel, sky and sea together. Humans usually deploy straight lines and rectangles, and flat slabs covered with a single color. Nature rarely does so.

A crossing started at dawn or before begins in a world of soft, impermanent forms and feathered edges. There is no firm floor, ceiling or walls. The sea, air and clouds all give way, if pressed. Colors swell and ebb, changing imperceptibly or suddenly, subtly or by surprise. Names for these colors prove far too simple – "blue" must embrace countless shifting hues and shades.

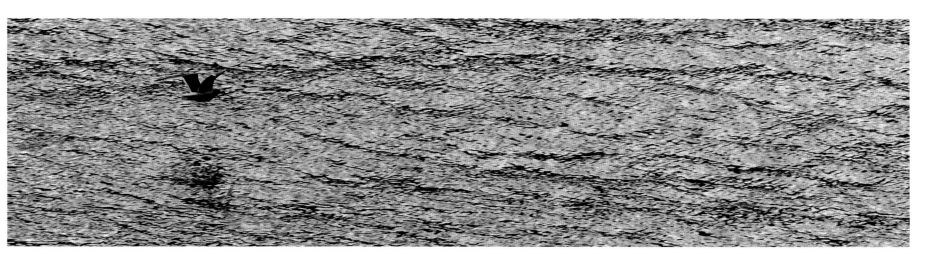

The fluidity of water is easily seen. Where the sea meets the air, its face mirrors light and so reveals its form. Its surface displays the waves made by a strong wind or boat wake, and riffles caused by the mildest breeze. The reflective lenses of the water change swiftly and incessantly. Air is even more fluid, but invisibly so.

Air and water present a traveling ferry with only token resistance, brief and yielding. The hard mass of the moving vessel cleaves the air, driving it up and to the sides. The boat's hull squeezes water outward, forcing the water to rise into wake waves as it moves away. The air and water are displaced and roiled for a time, but both flow fluidly back as the transient interruption passes.

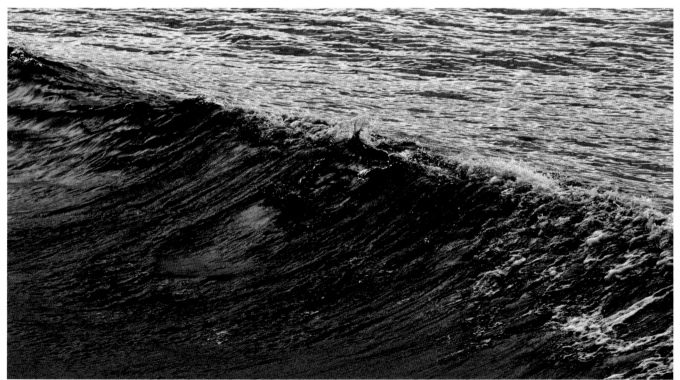

Facing page, top: A soft breeze turns the surface of the Sound into a slab of silver veined with gold.

Above: Parallel waves display dancing reflections from a sunset sky.

At left, and bottom of facing page: Ferries carve their wakes across the Sound, and the water foams, retreats, and then slides quickly back, like fine sand moving on the face of a dune.

There is little that is fluid about the forms of a ferry or a city's office towers.

A ferry's sharp lines, sheer slab sides and regular rows of openings show a close familial resemblance to the varying but repetitive planes of the window-walls facing the Sound from downtown Seattle.

The boat echoes a building that has been laid flat to allow it to sail on its side.

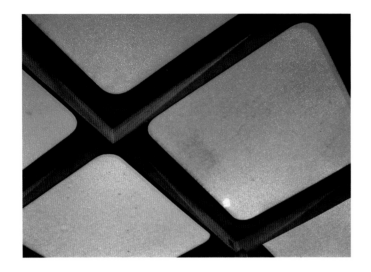

Forms aboard the ferries are sharply delineated, hard and regular, with all rust-prone metal plates thickly painted.

The linear markings of human activities abound not only in shapes aboard the ferry but also at times in the skies above.

The crisp and angular forms of the ferry's structural elements become the frame for the softer world surrounding a crossing.

Reflections on sailing from Seattle

For those who commute from the west side of the Sound to Seattle, the days begin and end with different rhythms and vistas.

In each direction, the commuter is traveling towards where the Sun rose or will rise, or has set or will later set. In some ways, commuters may have the best itinerary – they frequently will travel during the "golden hours" near dawn and dusk, when slanting light from the Sun touches Earth in special ways.

Those on different schedules, or simply taking the ferry as an outing, with no rigid constraints, more often will travel westward before returning east, and typically will make both trips in daylight hours. What they see on the Sound will differ accordingly.

At left: The Wenatchee, *in a Seattle-side slip,*
awaits departing passengers for a midday sailing.

Following pages, overleaf: Ferries sail from and to
Seattle at sunset, as seen from Bainbridge Island.

Views of the angular city skyline, the ferry terminal's surroundings and Elliott Bay offer themselves throughout the day to those boarding outbound ferries in Seattle.

Facing page: Condominiums and offices stand on the hills above the waterfront north of the Pier 52 ferry terminal.

At left and above: A ferry loads for a Seattle departure.

At left: Fire and rescue boats serving harbor traffic – here, the Chief Seattle – are stationed just north of the ferry terminal.

Below: Gulls are abundant around Pier 52.

Above: To the southeast, behind the container port's cranes, Mount Rainier's peak rises above a layer of urban haze.

At left: Seattle's Smith Tower, seen from a ferry in its slip, acts as a readily recognizable landmark near the ferry terminal. Completed for a typewriter tycoon in 1914, this 522-foot building housed 540 offices and was one of the first "skyscrapers" in the United States.

The port bustles with traffic. Harbor workers hoist containers on and off ships' decks with massive cranes, encircle boats with booms to contain accidental spills, and operate tugs to nudge huge vessels into and out of the docks.

At right: Bulk cargo – loose material like grains placed directly into holds – is handled at a facility with silos and conveyor belts north of Pier 52.

Following pages, overleaf: The twin projections at each end of the car ferries on the main deck level – extending over the car deck and called "pickleforks" – offer a vantage point for watching the Seattle terminal glide away behind the ferry. This view also shows the slip's "wingwalls" and "dolphins".

As the ferry leaves the Seattle terminal behind, the vistas widen to the north, east, and south. New sights come into view as the boat moves away to the west.

Following pages, overleaf:
On a clear day, a sailing
from Seattle may offer a
panorama of the Olympics.

107

Some physical components are present every day on the Sound – there is always the water, the city, a skyline. But the experience of those is not constant, and instead varies with the season, the hour, whims of weather, and the nature and quality of light that is illuminating the moment of time.

At left: Late-day sunlight bounces back onto the Sound from west-facing windows of office buildings.

Following pages, overleaf: As the ferry moves west across Elliott Bay, the view to the north includes the Space Needle and may add anchored cargo ships, the Cascades foothills, or another ferry.

A ferry sailing out of Seattle in the afternoon frequently moves towards a "late-day" sky with broken clouds and mixed tones and shadings of orange, gray, and blue.

In winter, "late day" comes early – the Sun disappears before 5:00 p.m. – but the long days of summer offer similar views much later.

For commuters, business hours between November and March often do not end before sunset. Their sailings from Seattle occur at dusk and under muted light or, in the depths of winter, well after dark.

The sinking Sun brings out headlights, a soft silhouette of The Brothers' peaks, and glowing windows on office towers. As the ferry pulls away from the city, cell phone callers seek unimpeded reception on the picklefork at the Seattle end of the boat.

When Seattle is left behind at dusk, the Sun sometimes will flash a brief farewell of warm tones to end the day.

Those in transit move through the boarding area of the terminal and down the walk-on ramp while vehicles load below.

The processes and rhythms of a ferry's loading do not change after dark, but night alters the moods around the terminal. The vistas to the west are gone, swallowed in rising darkness. Except where the orange or greenish-white glowing zones of man-made illumination reign, the world has been shadowed and simplified.

Some homeward-bound commuters who avoid the busy main deck gravitate to one of the two quiet "reading rooms" on the upper deck; others head for the open air of the covered solariums.

Commuters taking their habitual places on the ferry already may be seated while a full Moon slips up through the crevice between two office towers.

For a commuter, sailing from Seattle reverses the patterns of the morning journey to the east. Ramps ascended in the morning now are traveled in the opposite direction on the westerly return. As the ferry moves away from Seattle, the city is left behind in ways that are both physical and also spiritual. First the bustle and roar slip away, and often the stresses of the day as well, as the crossing nears its end and approaches home, somewhere ahead past the western shore.

Reflections on circles and cycles

The scenery of the Sound dances under a show of light that varies in response to a symphony of continuous natural change.

The Earth spins on its axis as it sweeps in an ellipse around the Sun, and the seasons shift almost imperceptibly each day as the sphere's tilt varies the exact angular relationship of the Earth and Sun. The tides follow the separate, asynchronous pulls of the Moon and the Sun, maintaining a tempo of ebb and flood that is distinctively their own. Circles whirl while they move inside and around other circles, and rhythmic waves and patterns cycle within them. What once was called "the music of the spheres" can still be heard on the Sound.

There, these forces can be seen at play across the mountain peaks, the layers of water and cloud, and the dome of the skies.

On the Sound, the northwest summer typically begins in early July and ends in late September. June may extend a brief preliminary glimpse of the sunny, warm, calm days to come, but seldom is that promise kept until after June has ended.

During the true summer, long daylight hours and the cumulative effects of so many successive warmer days alter the appearance of the Sound: A soft haze rises from the water and diffuses distant views; the skies lighten; the surface of the Sound turns to paler placid blues, as if forgetting the slate gray of winter and the blacker blues and greens of waters swept by streaming winds.

For those visiting during the peak tourism season, the Sound can create memories of muted blues, sunlight that is warm but not searing, and gentle, cool, moist air.

In summer, the ferry's open outer decks, almost entirely empty of people on sailings during the depths of winter, for a time will host individuals and groups intrigued by the sight of a passing tug or gravel barge, the skyline, outbound ships, or the simple pleasure of standing outside at an end of the boat in the sunshine and breeze as the ferry makes its way across the Sound.

Summers on Puget Sound bring many first-time visitors for whom a ride on a ferry is a novel outing. Unlike weekday commuters whose crossings may defy counting, those new to the experience of a ferry passage are typically intrigued by the mechanics of the boat's operations and by the Sound and what it reveals. That enthusiasm can remind long-time riders of what they have ceased to see, and how remarkable it is.

At right: Passengers watch from the upper deck walkway, one level above the dock-end picklefork, as a ferry prepares to enter its slip in Eagle Harbor.

As the ferry approaches the wingwalls that will cradle the slip-end nose of the boat, the dock-end propeller is used to slow the boat. The prop mixes air into the water, changing its color, creating an icing of white foam, and spinning out a whirling eddy.

At left: A late-afternoon ferry nears Bainbridge Island.

Below: The warm-weather haze and calm waters common in summer shape the views of Mount Rainier, bringing soft blues to the sky and surface of the Sound.

133

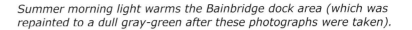

Summer morning light warms the Bainbridge dock area (which was repainted to a dull gray-green after these photographs were taken).

For westside commuters working in Seattle, summer provides welcome relief from pre-dawn sailings and homecomings after dark. By the time of peak morning commuting hours, the Sun has been up for hours. The morning light is orange with warmth, and both passages of the daily commute will occur during the golden hours of the day.

The Earth spins ever on, and each summer so must end. Between one sunrise and the next, Earth has moved 1.6 million miles on its annual trek around the Sun. A span of 580 million miles in space stands between the peak of summer and the next comparable day. For a commuter on the Seattle end of a ferry, sunrise comes only minutes later each day. The rotation between sunrises, at 1,000 miles an hour, offers a ready time-marker for a day. Too slow to sense, but too fast to grasp, this spinning sphere that seems so stable also is hurtling around the Sun at almost 67,000 miles an hour.

That incomprehensible speed tells another narrative of time – one that plays out on Earth as the seemingly slow pace of the cyclical seasonal change.

As the summer slips away, the colors of autumn will arrive, and the silver and gray palette of winter will not be far behind.

Autumn supplants a waning summer and then begins to transmute itself into winter. The sunrises seen from Eagle Harbor no longer take place directly behind Seattle's skyline. The Sun instead appears farther to the south each day, eventually adopting a low arc on the horizon, on the shortest day of the year never more than 23 degrees above the Sound. Soft blues and silvers of summer gradually give way to deeper hues of color, and various forms of fog begin to make their appearance, both on the Sound and in the basin along its shores, filling the valleys below the ranges of mountains.

With the passage of autumn into winter, cloud overcast and rain become steadily more common. Commutes again begin soon after sunrise, and then around sunrise, and, gradually, even before the sky has started to lighten.

Between autumn and spring, the Sun's lower elevation, the heavier clouds, increased storm activity, and occasional fog all add to the interplay of forces shaping the light. In the depths of winter, shades of silver, pewter and gray predominate in the sky and sea.

On some mornings, thick fog fills the air, or a thin broken blanket may cling close to the water. When visibility is reduced, some navigation aids will sound audible warnings, while ferries deploy their deep-toned "ship's whistle", adding a new element to a crossing.

Facing page: In mid-winter, clouds can blanket the Sound, and the Sun barely rises over the horizon to the south of Eagle Harbor.

At left: The Sun shines on Seattle despite fog overlaying the Sound.

Below: Moisture close to the comparatively warmer waters of the Sound condenses in the calm but icy air above.

Fog facts:

Several types of fog appear around the Sound. Fog often is nothing other than a "low cloud", but it can have other origins, forms and colloquial names.

In very cold calm air, the warmth radiating from the water at night causes a layer of cooler air to be trapped near the surface, holding suspended moisture and producing "radiation fog", while "steam fog" occurs when a mass of very cold air moves across over warmer land or waters.

"Ground fog" refers to a low-lying blanket of fog under clear skies, and "sea fog" is caused by water condensing on tiny airborne salt particles.

"Valley fog" can be held in place for hours or days when a layer of warm air lies atop a lower band of moist, colder air and traps the fog in a valley.

Mount Rainier is often the site of "upslope fog" – as winds drive moist air up into the cooler zones on the mountain's higher slopes, condensation forms and produces what appears from afar to be a "cap" atop the mountain (a lenticular cloud).

"Haze" that is natural (not caused by air pollution) is common in the basin of the Sound during the summer months, when evaporation into warm air is held there as minute droplets of moisture.

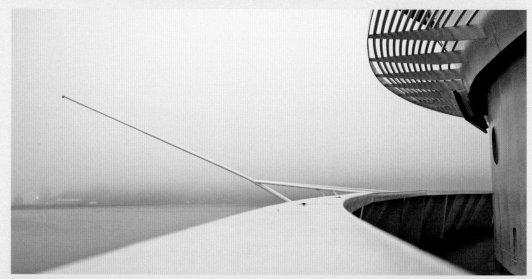

Clockwise from lower left, facing page:

Seen from the upper deck of a ferry, dense gray "low cloud" fog in Eagle Harbor masks everything beyond the ferry's jackstaff.

The orb of the Sun is clearly visible through a thin layer of "ground fog" over the Sound.

On Mount Rainier, winds driving moist air uphill produce "upslope fog" and a cloud cap. A cloud cap lingering above the mountain is said to be a predictor of coming rainy weather.

Above, soft fingers of "radiation fog" rise from waters along the shore of Bainbridge near dawn, before the Sun "burns off" the fog.

At left, a river of frigid air pouring down from the Olympics changes the layer of warmer, moist air close to the Sound's surface into "steam fog" at the mouth of Eagle Harbor.

Fog retains its form only in calm conditions.

Winter's shadings of gray range from as bright as silver and pewter to as dark as charcoal. Other hues, no matter how subtle, are enhanced by their contrast to those stark, dominant backgrounds.

151

The darkest days of deep winter are not without an occasional ironic gift for area residents: It is in winter, after an ice-cold, powerful storm has blown through, that the clarity of the air is at its best, and the skies and waters of the Sound are as blue as any imagining of summer might desire.

Mountain peaks half a hundred miles away are then on the doorstep of the Sound, capped with snow, and anyone who is not standing in the below-freezing air might mistake the vistas shown in a photograph taken then for a balmy summer scene. The slate days of winter are short and gray, but are relieved by such surprises.

Those crisp, crystalline days are rare in winter. During many consecutive weeks in January and February, Seattle lives up to at least part of a dreary reputation. A pall of gray lies low over the Sound.

Following pages, overleaf: The dull gray of a winter day seems to absorb all but the brightest man-made colors, like those on the containers being carried by this ship headed towards the cargo facilities on Harbor Island.

The annual transition from winter to summer is tumultuous. With increasing frequency as winter loses its hold, forceful storms sweep over the Sound, splitting the clouds open and exposing the Earth to skies that are clear, however briefly. A day may bring hail and tempestuous winds, or hours of dull overcast interspersed with glowing intervals of light.

The clouds of spring look to the past and future – they recall the heaviest dark winter blankets but, between their rows and towers, they hint about the coming clear blue days of summer.

Between March and June, spring storms shred the overcast and allow beams of light to pour down onto the Cascades and Olympics.

A late-afternoon spring storm front drives the western edge of the clouds into a line above the Olympics, allowing the distant sunset to glow through valleys among the mountains behind Eagle Harbor.

Reflections on the transit system

Along Seattle's waterfront, excursion boats offer tours of the Sound. The ferries have a different core function: They exist not for scenic outings, but as a way to transport vehicles and people from one place to another. For decades, if not for a century, talk of bridges across the water has been just talk; ferries still fulfill that role.

On both sides of Puget Sound, highways and streets funnel cars and buses to and from the ferry terminals. Traffic is concentrated there into a narrow stream. Ferry routes form slender links across the wide water. The alternative is a much longer drive around the shores of the Sound.

Clockwise from bottom:

At the Bainbridge Island terminal, an open ramp leads up from the bus transit area and connects with a long enclosed pedestrian walkway that runs from the terminal's front entrance downhill to the facility's two ferry slips.

Where these pathways meet, walk-on passengers converge from both areas and are then funneled into the final section of the elevated walkway system.

The route forms a long zig-zagging path to the ferry slips and incorporates a bridge that passes above the vehicle-loading ramp.

For vehicles, the car ferries are much like a tunnel, except that these tunnels also move. Cars drive into one entrance and, after stopping for a time, drive out the other end in a distant location. The ferry phrase "car tunnel" is thus peculiarly apt. For foot passengers, a ferry trip more closely resembles a bus ride, with both transit terminals and transfer points at either end.

Facts about Central Sound ferry routes:

The WSF "Sailing Schedule" provides timetables for the entire system. The Schedule's map, at right, shows all of the Puget Sound routes.

This map also depicts the eastern side of the Olympic Peninsula (on the Port Townsend side of a line drawn due north from Shelton) and the Kitsap Peninsula, to the east of the fish-hook shape of the Hood Canal, which separates the two peninsulas. The two bodies of water that wrap around the base of the Kitsap Peninsula – the Hood Canal and the northern end of Case Inlet – almost meet at a narrow neck of land where the circled "3" appears between Shelton and Bremerton.

The four primary commuting routes between the Seattle metropolitan area on the eastside and the western peninsulas start (in the north) with the Edmonds/Kingston route and reach down to include the Fauntleroy/Southworth route in the south. All four of these routes serving the Seattle area are essentially east-west transits. A fifth active ferry route for commuters – but transporting only foot passengers, not cars – runs between Seattle and Vashon Island.

Farther south, commuters in south Kitsap County or north Mason County traveling to Tacoma or to areas between Tacoma and Seattle have the option of using a bridge that spans the Tacoma Narrows.

The graphic at right, from the WSF website, is a "live" depiction of the locations of Central Sound ferries at about 5 p.m. on one October day. The blue markers indicate ferries in transit, while red markers show those docked in slips for disembarking and reloading. This map does not show the Edmonds/ Kingston route (north of Bainbridge Island).

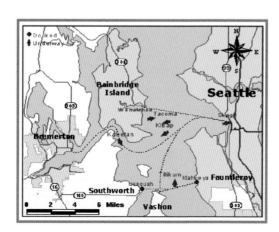

"Central Sound" is not a phrase with a fixed meaning. A WSF pass for Central Sound routes includes only those connecting to Bremerton, Bainbridge, and Kingston (on the westside). More generally, however, the phrase is used as a description for the part of Puget Sound extending roughly from Kingston in the north to Tacoma at the southern end.

During peak commuting hours, the proximity of several busy ferry routes in the central part of Puget Sound almost guarantees that passengers riding on one ferry are likely to see one or more other ferries making crossings on a different route.

The westside-eastside commute: There are five counties on the west side of the Sound with all or part of their populations within commuting distance of the Seattle metro area primarily because ferry service exists. Kitsap County is the most eastern of those counties, but parts of Clallam, Jefferson, Mason and Grays Harbor counties also extend close enough to a westside ferry terminal that some people living there are willing to take on the trek to a terminal and from there on across the Sound.

As Seattle expanded and its freeways clogged, increasing numbers of people drawn to the city's jobs sought to avoid other aspects of the sprawling metropolis. For them, the commute aboard a ferry was more attractive than spending the same time, or more, negotiating city-side traffic. And others, living along the eastern side of the Kitsap Peninsula anywhere between Bremerton and Kingston, or even farther away, were willing to travel over to Seattle even if that meant journeying to and from a ferry terminal each day, and then spending most of another hour (or more) each way within the ferry system.

Jobs are a primary force driving the flow of people. In the five westside counties, about 370,000 people live within commuting distance of the eastside – 240,000 on the Kitsap Peninsula and another 125,000 on the Olympic Peninsula. In those five westside counties, one job exists for every three people. The eastside is an employment magnet.

In King County, where Seattle is located, the population-to-jobs ratio drops to 1.7 to 1. The three main eastside counties (King, Pierce and Snohomish) hold 3 million people (half the State's population).

Bainbridge Island once was a semi-rural outpost considered to be far from Seattle in almost every respect, with small farms, forestry and fishing operations. The island also was a preferred location for many "getaway" vacation homes. The Island now is often seen as a suburb of Seattle or a bedroom community for that city, even though the Island is in Kitsap County.

Bainbridge's ferry terminal (in the Winslow village area) serves not only Island residents but also commuters from farther away. As a result, even though only about 23,000 people live on Bainbridge, the Island's population swells with commuters between 5:00 a.m. and 7:30 p.m. during the work-week. On weekdays ferries begin running from Bainbridge to Seattle as early as 4:45 a.m., and the last ferry returning to Bainbridge leaves Seattle each night around 1:35 a.m. The transit service pauses each night, but only for a few hours.

The commuter flow eastward to the city peaks each day between 6:00 and 8:45 a.m. Afternoon and evening sailings bring those passengers back westward from work, and the afternoon traffic is most heavily concentrated on ferries leaving Seattle between 4:30 and 6:30 p.m.

The Kaleetan, *traveling west from Seattle to Bremerton, draws close to the southern end of Bainbridge Island.*

Facts about the Seattle/Bainbridge route:

The sketch at right depicts the approximate route usually followed by ferries traveling between Seattle and Bainbridge Island, as well as water depths at selected locations.

Seattle's Elliott Bay is a true deep-water port, with the bottom shelving quickly to as deep as 200' only a few hundred feet offshore. The central north/south channel of the Sound midway between Seattle and Bainbridge is 600 to 800 feet deep (about as deep as the Sound gets).

Near Bainbridge, however, a spit that remains submerged except at very low tides runs roughly southeast from Wing Point, at the northern side of the entrance into Eagle Harbor. Almost a half mile offshore, the water depths at high tide are no more than 25 feet. A navigation channel along the eastern face of the Island follows a twisting path of deeper water into the harbor.

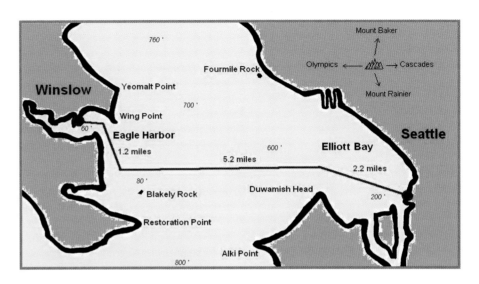

Above: The route between Seattle and the Bainbridge Island terminal follows a navigation channel along the Island's eastern shore. To avoid shallows south of Wing Point, ferries travel north and south in the area extending from the entrance to Eagle Harbor to about a mile south of the harbor.

At left: The Wing Point spit during a summer low tide, seen from inside Eagle Harbor looking east.

Safety announcements are played over the PA system after sailings begin. One variation describes the State's ferry system as among the "safest in the world". That may be true for the passengers, but it is not always so for ferry crew members. They shepherd tourists, regular commuters, baseball and football crowds, and occasional rowdies, ensuring that what needs to be done is done, and that the ferry trips are safe and adhere as closely as feasible to their schedules of sailings.

What can go wrong will do so; everything does not always run smoothly. On the vehicle deck, a car may fail to start, blocking all of the vehicles behind it. People have walked or driven off leaving behind their wallets, baggage, in-laws, visiting guests, and even children.

A habitual walk-on may forget having taken a car that day, and disembark leaving the car behind. Far too often, the crew members working on the car deck are hit by inattentive drivers who were busy on a cell phone or sending a text message, or simply careless.

For any ship of steel, the Sound is not a welcoming environment. Salt water, salt spray, and salty air attack iron in all its forms; the salt also heightens the conduction of electrical currents, so that two metals that are dissimilar interact in ways that can consume one, the other, or both. The mass of a ferry also means that damage is likely even from a slow grounding or contact with a breakwater or pier.

Hulls corrode and rust; continuous flexing stresses joints between the metal plates and frame components; engine parts wear out; and propellers and rudders can be bent or rendered useless if they strike a submerged object or a floating "deadhead" log.

Above and at right: The heavy car ramps and other slip facilities require periodic maintenance, and work may be done from a barge.

Facing page: A year before her scheduled 10-year major refit, the Puyallup *shows a rust-stained flank, and the fleet's constant struggle with corrosion, as she turns to head east to Seattle.*

Some maintenance requires using a drydock, and so must be accomplished in the Harbor Island facilities in Seattle. General maintenance for the ferry fleet is handled at the ferry yard located west of the terminal in Bainbridge Island's Eagle Harbor. And sometimes old boats are past the point of repair, and go there to die or, in gentler parlance, for "decommissioning".

For those who treasure their own experiences on the ferries, it brings sadness to see a once-proud ship facing out onto waters that she will never sail again.

The four "Steel Electric Class" ferries withdrawn from service in late 2007 were distinctive from the more modern boats, in ways other than the round "porthole" openings on their car decks: Smaller in size and with minimal draft, they were particularly suited for serving routes with lower levels of traffic demand and shallower or narrower harbors.

But 80 years of service and the stresses of all their labors took their toll. After 2007, the *Quinault, Nisqually, Illahee* and *Klickitat* most likely never will sail again carrying passengers. Moved to moorings in Eagle Harbor, they were doomed to spend their final time on the Sound watching newer, fresher craft ply those familiar waters.

One of the two WSF "Chinook/Snohomish *Class*" ferries crosses the bow of the Illahee on her way to a night berth in Eagle Harbor. These fast foot ferries are 143 feet long, carry 350 people (but no vehicles) and use water-jet propulsion to cruise at 38 knots.

Facing page and above: The Illahee, *built in 1927, awaits her decommissioning in Eagle Harbor.*

Most WSF routes are served by two ferries, which operate like a matched pair of slow pendulums that have been set swinging in synchronized but opposite arcs. One boat will be loading on the eastern side of the Sound while travelers board the other at the west-side terminal on the route's other end, and the two ferries will pass one another on the Sound in mid-route.

For passengers using either terminal on these routes, this allows a ferry to be available at intervals that are roughly the same for each route (although the intervals are different for each route, because of different sailing distances and demand). During peak weekday travel times, ferries depart from each terminal roughly every 30 minutes at Mukilteo and Clinton, every 40 to 45 minutes on the Edmonds/Kingston route, approximately every 50 minutes on the Seattle/Bainbridge route, and about every 80 minutes on the Seattle/Bremerton route.

The timing of the boats appears to be linear for a person looking down one column of the WSF "Sailing Schedule", but realizing that loading and unloading are synchronized on either side of the Sound changes the perceived rhythm.

Facts about the rhythm of the ferries:

The WSF "Sailing Schedule" provides key salient information. As shown below, it quickly answers the most basic, pragmatic question, "Which departure fits my schedule?"

What is not obvious from a quick glance at one part of the schedule is the cyclic rhythm that drives the boats each day.

Seattle / Bainbridge Island
Crossing Time: Approximately 35 minutes

Monday through Friday
Leave Seattle

5:30	10:40	3:45	9:00
6:10	11:25	4:40	10:05
7:05	12:20	5:30	10:55
7:55	1:10	6:20	12:15
8:45	2:05	7:20	1:35
9:35	3:00	8:10	

Leave Bainbridge Island

4:45	9:40	2:55	8:10
5:20	10:25	3:50	8:55
6:20	11:30	4:35	9:45
7:05	12:20	5:30	11:35
7:55	1:10	6:30	12:55
8:45	2:05	7:10	

For the Seattle/Bainbridge route, as an example, looking at what is occurring at both terminals at the same points in time – with one additional bit of information – tells a more complete story about the two-way patterns of ferry traffic, a view not readily apparent from the perspective of a passenger in transit who is seeing only half of what is happening on the route.

The schedule hints, but does not explain, that both ferries serving this route are moored in Eagle Harbor at night. This causes the first sailing from Bainbridge (at 4:45 a.m.) to become – after it offloads and reloads in Seattle – the first sailing back across to Bainbridge (at 5:30 a.m.).

By 6:15 a.m., the harmony of the rhythm is almost established.

From 7:05 a.m. until 8:10 p.m., the two ferries are leaving the opposite-end terminals at times that are very closely synchronized throughout most of the primary travel hours of a day.

Longer turnaround times at each terminal are built into the schedule for the peak travel periods when loading and unloading cars and people typically take longer than 15 minutes, the time allocated for that during most of the day.

If the sailing chronologies for the "yellow boat" (the first to start) and the "blue boat" (the second to begin its rounds) are overlaid, the pattern of their schedules, like the actual ferries, crosses in the middle throughout the day. Two matching, rhythmic waves dance within a sailing schedule. Adding the perspective of passing time, their motion is a spiraling helix.

Morning to mid-afternoon sailings

"BOAT 1"				"BOAT 2"			
Leaves Winslow	Arrives Winslow	Arrives Seattle	Leaves Seattle	Leaves Winslow	Arrives Winslow	Arrives Seattle	Leaves Seattle
4:45 a.m.							
	5:20 a.m.			5:20 a.m.			
			5:30 a.m.				
						5:55 a.m.	
	6:05 a.m.						6:10 a.m.
6:20 a.m.							
					6:45 a.m.		
		6:55 a.m.					
			7:05 a.m.	7:05 a.m.			
	7:40 a.m.					7:40 a.m.	
7:55 a.m.							7:55 a.m.
		8:30 a.m.			8:30 a.m.		
			8:45 a.m.	8:45 a.m.			
	9:20 a.m.					9:20 a.m.	
9:35 a.m.							9:35 a.m.
		10:10 a.m.			10:10 a.m.		
			10:40 a.m.	10:40 a.m.			
	11:15 a.m.					11:15 a.m.	
11:30 a.m.							11:25 a.m.
		12:05 p.m.			12:00 p.m.		
			12:20 p.m.	12:20 p.m.			
	12:55 p.m.					12:55 p.m.	
1:10 p.m.							1:10 p.m.
		1:45 p.m.			1:45 p.m.		
			2:05 p.m.	2:05 p.m.			
	2:40 p.m.					2:40 p.m.	
2:55 p.m.							3:00 p.m.
		3:30 p.m.			3:35 p.m.		
			3:45 p.m.	3:50 p.m.			

Mid-afternoon to late-night sailings

"BOAT 1"				"BOAT 2"			
Leaves Winslow	Arrives Winslow	Arrives Seattle	Leaves Seattle	Leaves Winslow	Arrives Winslow	Arrives Seattle	Leaves Seattle
			3:45 p.m.	3:50 p.m.			
	4:20 p.m.					4:25 p.m.	
4:35 p.m.							4:40 p.m.
		5:10 p.m.			5:05 p.m.		
			5:30 p.m.	5:30 p.m.			
	6:05 p.m.					6:05 p.m.	
6:30 p.m.							6:20 p.m.
		7:05 p.m.			6:55 p.m.		
			7:20 p.m.	7:10 p.m.			
	7:55 p.m.					7:45 p.m.	
8:10 p.m.							8:10 p.m.
		8:45 p.m.			8:45 p.m.		
			9:00 p.m.	8:55 p.m.			
	9:35 p.m.					9:30 p.m.	
9:45 p.m.							10:05 p.m.
		10:20 p.m.			10:40 p.m.		
			10:55 p.m.	Boat stays in Winslow until next morning			
	11:30 p.m.						
11:05 p.m.							
		12:10 a.m.					
			12:15 a.m.				
	12:50 a.m.						
12:55 a.m.							
		1:30 a.m.					
			1:35 a.m.				
2:05 a.m.							
Boat stays in Winslow until next morning							

Above: The Seattle/Bainbridge Island weekday sailing schedule, recast to show arrival times and contemporaneous activities at each terminal.

179

Below: As the Hyak *arrives at Seattle, her windows hurl late-afternoon summer light back onto the Sound.*

Facing page: Loading in a slip on Bainbridge Island, the Puyallup *reflects mid-morning summer light.*

The Rhythm of the Ferries

Sailing
  away from Seattle,
    a ferry travels west,
      the Cascades astern,
        the Olympics ahead.
          Out on Puget Sound,
            midway in the voyage,
              two travelers glide past each other,
                crossing
            side to side, each on its own voyage,
          heading to the City,
        carrying people east,
        moving into Elliott Bay,
      the City skyline rising,
    water churning ahead
  as it closes with the dock.
The ferry offloads,
but is refilled again
with cars and people.
  Then sailing
    away from Seattle,
      a ferry travels west,
        the Cascades astern,
          the Olympics ahead.
          Out on Puget Sound,
            midway in the voyage,
              two travelers glide past each other,
                crossing
            side to side, each on its own voyage,
          heading to the City,
         carrying people east,
        moving into Elliott Bay,
      the City skyline rising,
    water churning ahead
  as it closes with the dock.
The ferry offloads,
but is refilled again
with cars and people.
  Then sailing
    .....

                Sailing
              from the Island,
            a ferry travels east,
          the Olympics astern,
        the Cascades ahead.
      Somewhere around
    the halfway point,
  going to the Island,
  carrying people west,
  passing Blakely Rock
    and slowing to turn
      into Eagle Harbor.
  Nestled within the slip,
    the ferry empties,
      until new travelers
      people its decks again.
           Then sailing
              from the Island,
            a ferry travels east,
          the Olympics astern,
        the Cascades ahead.
      Somewhere around
    the halfway point,
  going to the Island,
  carrying people west,
  passing Blakely Rock
    and slowing to turn
      into Eagle Harbor.
  Nestled within the slip,
    the ferry empties,
      until new travelers
      people its decks again.
           Then sailing
        .....

Reflections on a myriad of mirrorings

Echoes of light and form reverberate around the Sound. The sky and water touch, light strokes both, and something new is sparked. Patterns arise in ripples that have rolled from invisible shores. Shapes embody symmetries and engage in mimicry, or mirror one another indirectly by their contrasts. Even human actions cycle back like reflected waves.

Passing turbulence forms soft mirrors in the eastbound and westbound wakes of the "big turn", with the wake of each ferry reflecting different light and water conditions.

The waters of the Sound are transformed by the slant of light, by the absence or intensity of wind, by the form and color of what they reflect, and by the smallest paddle-tracks of waterfowl and the deep churning and rolling wakes of a vessel's propulsion.

On a sunset sailing from Seattle, the ferry's passage is remembered in its wake, and the wake in turn reflects the hues of the late-day sky and the lights of the container port.

From left: The Sound sparkles in the pilot house window of the Wenatchee; above the Columbia Tower, light from the Sun is returned by a waxing Moon; and the shadow of a reader outside on deck replicates the silhouetted form of a reader inside the ferry's "library".

The structure of a double-ended ferry creates symmetries throughout the boat. Each end is identical. There are two pilot houses, two car tunnel portals, and matching ramps at either end. From outside, where internal configuration variations are invisible, such a ferry sliced across halfway along its length would divide into two matched halves; likewise, sliced from end-to-end down the boat's centerline, the two pieces could be placed side-by-side and would appear to be virtually identical. Cut both ways from above into four quadrants, the ferry, like a sliced pie, would yield four matching, almost indistinguishably mirroring parts. The Sound's varying panoramas are displayed around those fixed symmetries.

On two different clear winter days, views to the west from the middle of the Sound are framed by the matching opposite upper side decks of the ferry. In both photographs, the low-lying band of land below the peaks of the Olympics Range is the central part of the eastern face of Bainbridge Island, the section between Blakely Harbor and Eagle Harbor.

On the facing page, a ferry from Seattle is just north of Blakely Harbor, and is about to make its turn to the north. On this page, Eagle Harbor is directly above this caption.

On the contrasting shorelines of Kitsap County and King County, separated by eight miles of water, the curved profiles of forested hillsides mirror the shapes of city hillsides forested with buildings.

Seattle and Bainbridge face one another across the Sound, with the Island taking the light frontally in the morning and the city throwing reflections to the west in the afternoon.

One day or moment may mirror another with the angle or tone of light, in the colors reflected on the Sound, or through a coincidence of movement or position.

Facing page: Light from the setting Sun highlights the plating along the side of the Tacoma *as she awaits passengers at the Seattle terminal.*

At left: By late spring, the Sun is rising far enough to the north for morning light to touch the normally shaded north side of a ferry in its slip on Bainbridge Island.

The most consistent mirror, the surface of the Sound, is also the most variable.   There are rare days of calm so still that the water resembles old rippled glass. Dancing puffs of a faint breeze alter reflections in ways that differ from the effects of a steadier wind.   The water adopts and amends the colors of the sky, the shapes of clouds, and the forms of shoreline objects.

Below: As an afternoon ferry arrives at Bainbridge Island on a windstill day, the sheltered waters of Eagle Harbor mirror the sunset skies above.

Facing page: A whim of late-day northwestern winter light pours a fluid layer of iridescent blue onto the textured waters west of Elliott Bay.

Seen from the Bainbridge Island shore south of Eagle Harbor, two ferries on the Seattle/Bainbridge route have passed one another mid-Sound.

The Tacoma, *in the foreground, is voyaging west towards Bainbridge.* The Puyallup, *closer to Seattle, is headed east into Elliott Bay.*

Reflections on Mount Rainier

Locally, Mount Rainier often is identified only as "the Big Mountain" or even simply as "the Mountain". Its cone towers above the horizon to the south-southeast of Seattle. Even in summer, its peak is capped with snow and ringed by glaciers

On a brilliant morning with temperatures still in the high 20s, only one stalwart passenger ventures onto the open front end of the upper deck of the Wenatchee *to contemplate the view of Mount Rainier as the ferry sails out of Eagle Harbor.*

The mountain is indifferent to our regard.
It has seen millions of dawns.

Facts about Mount Rainier:

Mount Rainier stands 68 miles south-southeast of Seattle. It is an active but dormant volcano with a current height of about 14,411 feet – "current" because the mountain blew off some 1,500 to 2,000 feet of its summit about 5,000 years ago, and "about" because its height is fluid, with the peak presently rising fractions of an inch each year as the Juan de Fuca tectonic plate is ground under and presses up against the western edge of the Continental plate.

Rainier was built about a million years ago through repeated eruptions and lava flows. It could erupt again at any time, like California's Lassen Peak in 1914 - 1921 and as Mount Saint Helens did in 1980.

Rainier is the fifth tallest mountain in the lower, contiguous 48 states, after Mount Whitney (in California) and Mounts Elbert, Masive, and Harvard (in Colorado). Those peaks surpass Rainier in height only by relatively small amounts, respectively 94, 29, 17 and 16 feet. Rainier once was taller than all of them.

Three distinct summits stand atop the cone of Mount Rainier. "Liberty Cap" (the lowest of the three) is located above the mountain's northwest face, and thus is visible from ferries crossing the Central Sound. For observers on the ferries and for others situated north and northwest of Rainier, the other two peaks – "Point Success" and "Columbia Crest" – are hidden behind Liberty Cap.

Use of the phrase "big mountain" to identify Rainier is hardly new. The mountain was known as "Tahoma" and by other similar names among Native Peoples – with those names interpreted to mean "big mountain" or "snowy peak". The English-language name was assigned by Captain George Vancouver during his coastal charting voyage after the peak was sighted from waters offshore of the Olympic Peninsula on May 8, 1792, with the name chosen to honor Rear Admiral Peter Rainier.

The mountain's base covers about 100 square miles. Rainier has 25 named glaciers and 34 to 36 square miles of glaciers – a greater glacial ice load than any other one mountain in the contiguous 48 states.

Each year on average, some 20 to 30 earthquakes occur deep in the Earth under Rainier. It at present is the second most seismically active volcano in the Cascades (after Mt. St. Helens).

Rainier is considered to be the potentially most dangerous volcano in that range because of its proximity to densely settled areas and its mass. Geologists believe there have been three collapses from the cone during the last 6,000 years. In the post-glacial era, there also have been at least 60 lahars – floods of water, mud, gravel and ice that race down the mountain's slopes and inundate all that the torrent does not sweep away.

When Rainier last lost part of its summit, the blast spread an estimated 0.7 cubic mile of material into the areas around the mountain. Eruptions and lahars from Rainier have shaped the Puget Sound basin and shoreline out to distances as far away as 60 miles from the mountain.

A meditation on Mount Rainier:

In late summer after August, when the snow and ice on Rainier's lower slopes have melted, a cone of white still tops the mountain. To the west, the highest peaks of the Olympics may then be gray rocky crags, entirely bare of snow. Rainier's white crown thus defines the altitude where ice always reigns – a "snowline" of unremitting cold that starts above the Olympics' nearly 8,000 foot heights.

The troposphere is about 10 miles deep – in comparison to the Earth's 8,000 mile diameter, that 10 miles represents only 0.00125. On a very large peach – say, a four-inch peach – a skin that was proportionately as thin as the troposphere would be only 5/1,000ths of an inch thick, a bit thicker than the average diameter of human hair. Stated another way, if an average-thickness human hair were wrapped around that peach, the hair would be about 80 percent as thick as the proportionate thickness of the layer of air constituting Earth's 10-mile troposphere.

But humans of course do not inhabit the entire 10-mile height of the troposphere – we reach our limits, rare exceptions aside, well below that. There are communities in the altitude zone between 10,000 and 15,000 feet, but they are few in number. For all but a small portion of humanity, sustained life above 10,000 feet would be a daunting challenge, if not impossible. Below that level – the level of the Rainier snowline – is the primary zone of life for humans and almost all animals and plants. Even if a 15,000 foot elevation is regarded as the upper boundary for human life, the fragile breathing skin of Earth, the zone in which we live, is about one-fourth as thick as a human hair held next to that large imagined peach.

The skin of a peach is famously fragile – and everything is relative, one often hears. The zone of life, the habitable atmosphere relative to the size of the Earth, is almost infinitesimally shallow, and much softer than the skin of a peach.

Humans inhabit the lowlands. There is a narrow layer for life between Rainier's peak and the sea level surface of the Sound. That is what the mountain's white summer snowline teaches.

Reflections on northwestern light

Throughout a year, there are pre-dawn sailings, passages that head to and away from sunrises and sunsets, and late-night and mid-day crossings, but the clockwork regularity of the ferries controls none of the greater variables.

Even if on one day the Sun stands in the sky precisely where it was a year ago, so that a 6:20 p.m. ferry once again departs Seattle in perfect harmony with the Sun's upper rim disappearing below the Olympics, the weather on the Sound seldom repeats itself except during the summer.

In other seasons, the basin is capricious. Some days bring unexpected mixes of sunshine and dense clouds, and rain, hail or snow. A routine daily commute passes through the regular change of seasons, and also into the unpredictable transformations brought about by the specific conditions of a particular day.

Between the blue-sky days of summer and the grayest days of winter, the predominant weather patterns feature soft overcasts that filter and diffuse the sunlight.

At times, there are sudden or slow-moving openings among or in the clouds, or even under them. Bright beams of sunlight may fleetingly pour through. Even then, the Sun's rays are angled obliquely, so that any direct light flowing down onto the Sound slants in from one side and sometimes falls invisibly somewhere far away.

Openings in the clouds often are edged with an inner radiance. Above the clouds, the sky appears as a cool and remote pale blue. Below the broken overcast, the Sound shows the blues, silvers, and grays of open shade.

The colors most commonly seen on silver-gray days like this are studies in pastels, subtle and nuanced. The clouds and sea are illuminated by a mellow inner glow that has settled like mist and was then absorbed by the features of the Earth.

The light at times appears to emanate from within the sea or sky, and even from inside steel. Muted tones of whites and greens meet soft brushstrokes of angled sunlight.

The clouds and the surface of the Sound may echo one another, sharing shadings of pewter, silver or gold, so that the water shimmers like a textured, satin sheet of burnished metal.

The late-day skies between October and June show fluid, muted hues.

Scenes that might otherwise be so familiar as to be stale are transformed by whimsical changes of the light, passing paintings in the sky, or by the happenstance occurrence of a window into blue through layers of clouds.

The Sound also knows how to display varieties of blue without reaching through the clouds. There are the blues of a clear day, soft blues at dusk, and, occasionally, a dark wash of blue that fills the air around the Sound.

One of the Sound's surprises is how quickly a scene can change. A traveler on a ferry who is watching a passing object may see it swiftly shift through ranges of light as the ferry moves, or as the observed object moves, or as both move at once in parallel or in opposite directions.

On a winter morning passage, with the Sun still low in the southeast, a ferry traveling west is shown in two images from less than two minutes apart. Above, the ferry is riding under dark clouds on silver and black seas. At right, moments later, it is sailing on green seas into a sunbreak.

At last light, shadows rise from the Earth as its face spins to the east away from the Sun. Heights are briefly highlighted, and then slip down into the climbing darkness.

The interval between the first hint of dawn and last gleam of a day is infused with varied and often fleeting displays of the northwest's special light.

Reflections on the "trackless sea"

The proposition that the passage of a vessel leaves no trace is a simplification that has become less true over time. It was far more accurate in the days of sail, when smaller vessels without internal combustion engines and propellers plied the seas. In another sense as well, routes across water have become less trackless because of developments in navigation methods and systems.

The "trackless seas" simplification is frequently inaccurate for the sheltered waters of the Sound.

Out on the open oceans, wave action is seldom absent, and waves or winds soon obliterate visible evidence of a ship's recent presence. Within the Sound on calm days, however, the water for hours afterwards carries on its surface the sheen left by the turbulence that a spinning propeller generates. Air was mixed into the water; the aerated water is lighter and so rises, and its surface tension has been transformed. It then floats in altered form as a shining record of the long-departed ship, until it can be dispersed by the wind or reabsorbed into the mass of water. On Puget Sound, ship tracks often linger on for hours after a vessel has passed.

Residual ship tracks are shown in the left-hand image on the preceding pages and, on these pages, in Eagle Harbor (above at right) and on Elliott Bay (at right) between the fogbank and the ferry outbound from Seattle.

On the facing page, two ferries sailing out of Seattle create fresh turbulence trails, and the pattern of ripples just below the left-hand ferry shows the waves created by that ferry's displacement wake.

Ships join other forces that sculpt the water's surface. Powers other than propellers are at play. Winds brush across the Sound, leaving behind marks as inconspicuous as small ripples and as evident as white-crested waves. Shimmering slicks form downwind of shoreline obstacles that impede a brisk breeze. Fresh rainwater floats atop denser salt water, and flows in visible streams from the shores. Tides and currents interact, with upwellings and eddies that alter the visible texture of the seas. There are localized variations for each element, so that enclosed bays and open waters differ.

The "V" of a ship's wake, like other fluid waves, creates secondary waves when the wake reaches and flows back from a shore, with reflecting waves leaving the shore again in a new direction and colliding with other waves. Two vessel wakes meeting at an angle form a new line of taller waves. The ripples in the pond of the Sound from all these forces are at work throughout the day, and they change the water's surface from a potentially flat monotone plane into a shimmering account of what has gone before, a memory of time and movement.

234

Facing page: Oblique light brings different tones to slicks in the center of the Sound where ship trails persist, and a ferry leaves a roiled green wake.

Above: The Tacoma is reflected only in the water her propeller has churned and transformed into a glassy mirror.

At left: Dark dashed wave lines mark where two wakes are meeting at an angle, but also are left by the unusual double displacement wakes of the many tugboats active on Elliott Bay.

235

Facts about ships and shipping:

Captain Vancouver and his ship *Discovery* arrived to chart the Northwest Coast with a crew of 99 jammed into that vessel's 95-foot length. Modern ships were, until recently, built to squeeze into the locks of the Panama canal. The "Panamax" limit for length was 965 feet and just under 106 feet for beam-width.

For years, container ships (sometimes called "box boats") adhered to those dimensions, while tankers and bulk-cargo vessels ("bulkers") were shorter to accommodate the standardized facilities in many ports – still with a 106-foot beam, but usually less than 750 feet long. In 1996, the first of the "Post-Panamax" container ships made its appearance, at 1,140 feet in length, and even larger "coast to coast" vessels subsequently have been built.

Worldwide, about 6,800 container ships and 6,200 "bulkers" are in use. Ships seen frequently on the Sound include "box boats" and "bulkers" as well as small tankers, barges serving local functions (including hauling containers from and to other ports around the Sound), occasional naval vessels, and, more recently, regular spring-to-fall cruise ships. Ships from the South Korean Hyundai and Hanjin lines cross paths with those from China's national fleet (China Ocean Shipping Corporation – COSCO) and of other nations (such as the Danish Maersk line).

At left: A specialty car carrier and a container ship head south to Tacoma, as seen from a ferry passing astern.

Along routes in the shallower waters of the Sound, deeper-water channels are delineated by navigation markers. These include moored floating buoys and placards on posts sunk into the bottom. Ferry passengers destined for Eagle Harbor can see the red markers pass on the right-hand side of the ferry as it adheres to the "red right returning" rule (keeping all the red markers to starboard – and green markers to port – when entering harbors). Charts and electronic gear including GPS systems now make navigation more certain. Ferries often sail under the control of a computer.

In the era of sail, before masters could communicate directly through ship-to-ship radios, a system of traffic rules developed – the "rules of the road" – with the prime goal of avoiding vessel collisions. The sea does not welcome lane-striping or signs declaring "yield" or "stop", and ships neither turn nor stop quickly. A 600-foot ship traveling at 11 knots cannot stop in less than 1.25 miles. When one vessel detects another within the zone of danger, five blasts of the ship's whistle will sound a precautionary warning.

The Tacoma *passes channel markers as she travels north along Bainbridge's eastern shore heading towards Eagle Harbor.*

Vessels under sail in theory have the right-of-way, but it would be imprudent for a sailor to insist upon claiming that priority over the Tacoma.

241

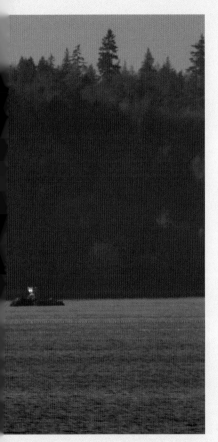

At left: The Tacoma, *voyaging west from Seattle towards Bainbridge Island, approaches Blakely Rock (marked with a navigation placard and light) and the point where the ferry will make the "big turn" to travel north along the Island's eastern shore on the route into Eagle Harbor*

Below: A closer view of Blakely Rock with the Bainbridge shore behind it.

Seen from the north, the Wenatchee, *bound for Seattle from Bainbridge, begins making her turn to the east well before she reaches Blakely Rock.*

Reflections on personal passages

No passenger riding a ferry across Puget Sound shares the exact experience of another traveler. Each takes a private journey in a public place.

Although the ferries are a transit system, they are not at all like a van, bus, or the crowded coach-seat rows of an airplane. On a ferry, behavior and personal choices are not so constrained. Options abound – different types and locations of seating, large spaces to explore, places for both privacy and collegiality. Each day, commuters define their transit experience by choosing where and with whom they will spend their time on a crossing, and what use they will make of the journey.

Above: Walk-ons navigate the long passageways to the ferries.

Facing page: Many make their daily working commute to and from Seattle on bicycles, rain or shine, throughout the year.

A passenger's form of transportation controls the entry-point to the ferry. Walk-ons follow passageways and ramps forming the boarding route to the gangway resting on one of the ferry's pickleforks. All cars, trucks and bicyclists are channeled below.

After boarding, all travelers are free to explore the boat, join the majority of riders inside the sheltered main deck, or go "outside" by ascending to the open upper deck.

Facts about the deck levels on ferries:

Conceptually, the WSF inland waters drive-on/drive-off car ferries have three levels – the car deck, open to the air at both ends and along the ship's sides; the fully-enclosed main passenger deck; and the upper deck (often described as the "sun deck").

Beyond those core similarities, the exact configuration of a WSF car ferry depends primarily on its size – the largest boats in the fleet offer features and areas (particularly on the upper deck) that cannot be accommodated on most smaller vessels.

On all double-ended ferries, matched pilot houses stand on the upper deck at each end of the vessel. The "front" pilot house is used to control the ferry when it travels in one direction; as the ferry unloads and reloads, the vessel's master moves to the other end of the boat, where the other pilot house is about to become the "front" one for the next voyage. On the largest WSF ferries (such as the *Puyallup*, shown at left), the twin pilot houses are located one level higher than the upper deck.

On those boats, the elevated position of the pilot houses makes room on the upper deck for spaces that can be open to passengers. On "Jumbo Mark II Class" boats (the *Puyallup*, *Tacoma* and *Wenatchee*) the upper deck contains a fully-enclosed passenger space and an area that is covered but open to the air at its end facing the boat's center. Those two areas are shown in the photograph at left on the upper deck aft of the pilot house.

The upper decks of "Jumbo Class" ferries (the *Spokane* and *Walla Walla*) provide a partially open covered seating area, but less generous upper-deck passenger areas. Spaces on the upper decks of some smaller ferries are accessible for passengers to explore, but some of these boats offer no outside seating.

The level below the upper deck, the fully enclosed main deck, is on the same level as the "pickleforks" where walk-on passengers board and disembark (at left, where the group of people is standing at the forward end of the boat). On the main-deck level, the decks at each end extend on each side to create a place where the gangway can be placed for foot traffic to board, but the decks are cut away in the center (over the vehicle tunnel). Viewed from above, the deck thus resembles a two-pronged, blunt-ended fork. Inside, the main deck is completely sheltered from the elements, with soft-cushioned chairs, booths, and a galley that serves refreshments and light meals.

The car deck on the larger ferries in fact consists of two levels – the overhead in the central area (the "tunnel") is high enough to clear the rooftops of even the largest highway trucks, and that leaves room on the sides for two stacked auto areas with lower ceilings, accessed by one-lane ramps up and down from the main car deck at either end of the boat. In the photograph at left, the two lowest lines of rectangular openings along the hull of the *Puyallup* show the locations of the ferry's two stacked car-deck levels along the boat's sides.

The various decks are accessible via interior stairways (on ships, often called "ladders") and by elevators (on most WSF ferries). Four external stairways at the ends (one on either side of the ferry) allow disembarking passengers to move quickly from the top deck down to the pickleforks.

On the largest ferries, the covered open-air sections on the upper deck just inboard of the pilot houses (the "solariums") have ceilings of glass panels and provide outdoor seating with protection from rain or spray, and some shielding from the wind.

The fully-enclosed areas on the upper deck – located closer to the boat's center – (also present only on the largest ferries) offer the option of interior seating away from the main passenger cabin. These areas have very limited views (they face the solariums) and are governed by a system of etiquette that regular riders have established over time. They are called the "reading rooms" or "libraries", and in those spaces allowing a cell phone to ring or engaging in anything other than the briefest hushed conversation will quickly draw disapproving looks.

The most crowded sailings carry the largest contingents of daily commuters. These regulars have their preferences: particular places on the boat or one person, or a group of acquaintances, with whom the transit will be shared. Some commuters work together on the city side; others are social familiars on the west side. Some who drive on never leave their vehicles, working, resting, or listening to music or a radio. Those who seek an assurance of quiet can go into one of the two upper "libraries" where a protocol of near silence reigns.

As they board, many commuters move quickly to a chosen and familiar spot, lest it be claimed first by someone else. For some, the location of preference is the row of seats at the very "front" of the boat as it travels to Seattle.

Clockwise from bottom of facing page: The "front row seats" of the main cabin; the rear library on the upper deck; a morning greeting as passengers board; a booth in the main passenger cabin; and a view out the car deck tunnel from a ferry in Eagle Harbor facing east towards Wing Point and Seattle.

On early morning crossings and chilly winter days, there are often only a few who leave the sheltered parts of the ferry to visit the exposed outer perimeter of the upper deck or its partially enclosed solariums. Those who do so may see the first hints of dawn in the sky or, once the boat has sailed, the Olympics astern or the city across the Sound.

For a small number of commuters, the upper deck is their only chosen place for all their passages. What beckons them may be the call of the open sky, avoiding the noises and crowd of the main deck, the feel and sounds of the wind, or the ability to move freely around the boat. Whatever their reasons, they will gravitate there almost every day, despite any inclement weather and seating that is limited to hard, weatherproof metal benches.

Whether trying to read a newspaper despite a breeze, prepare for work, or greet the day with music or a bottle of water and doing the crossword puzzle on the rail, they are out of doors.

For those commuters who will spend the balance of their working day within the confines of a building, their time on the upper deck during a cross-Sound passage is a change, if not a reprieve.

The upper deck's outer perimeter offers an exercise oval, for those so inclined. Along the ferry's sides, the outer deck can accommodate three people abreast. At the ends of the boat, above the car tunnel entrances, the walkway narrows and curves back in a semicircle.

On the largest ferries, a full circuit of the deck covers about 850 feet. Circling it six times means walking almost a mile. Some of those exercising use the ladders at each end, going down to the picklefork, across the end of the ferry, and back to the top deck on the other side.

The eastern end of a Seattle-bound ferry in an Eagle Harbor slip points straight at the city. An embarking passenger moving to that end of the boat on the upper deck can stand on the curved walkway above the car tunnel entrance and look out past the ferry's jackstaff and the silhouetted trees on Wing Point. If the timing is right, the sky may be hinting about the colors of the coming dawn, or already revealing them.

The deck shudders underfoot from the distant working of machinery deep in the hull as the ferry's "aft" propeller spins just fast enough to keep the boat's opposite end thrust against the wingwalls that form the docking bay.

Moments before departure, the engine below is ramped down when the last passengers have boarded and the propeller's stabilizing force is no longer needed. There is a pause of quiet, before the land-end engine of the ferry rumbles into action and begins to drive the boat away from the slip and to the east.

As the ferry accelerates, whatever natural breeze has been blowing over the eastern end of the ferry is amplified, suppressed, or redirected, as the new apparent wind created by the ferry's movement begins to increase in force.

Each day offers its own greeting of sky, sea and light.

On different mornings, a ferry may set out under a sky just blushing with the faint first rose shades of dawn, or under already brilliant clouds that could soon turn gray.

The open outer decks offer the most intense sensory experience of a crossing. In addition to the open sky, there will be wind. Even on a calm day, the effect of the boat's 18-knot cruising speed cannot be ignored; when that combines with wind blowing from ahead, walking on the upper deck with or against the gale can be a challenge. At places where the ferry is sweeping the air around its rounded "front" end, the force is like that in a powerful wind-tunnel – walking becomes reeling, or leaning forward, or trying not be blown along.

And there is sound: The wind shrieks across the railings in a chaotic chorus of flutes and piccolos, piping in varied tones without any evident harmony, but exhilarating and somehow still pleasing.

For some, claiming an early spot on the foredeck is not motivated solely by schedules. When the passage ends, they will disembark with others whose experiences of the crossing were different and equally their own.

Reflections on a single crossing

On a temperate day in February, a ferry sailed from Seattle at about 4:40 p.m., as scheduled. As occurs for every sailing, many walked west along the Marion Street trestle and then under Seattle's noisy Alaskan Way viaduct to enter the terminal on Pier 52. On that day, for that sailing, the interval of time between passing under that viaduct and stepping out onto the long ramp at the Bainbridge Island terminal was 62 minutes.

The photographs in this final section, including on the facing page, depict some fragments of what travelers saw or could have seen during those 62 minutes between entering and leaving the boundaries of the ferry system.

Nothing extraordinary or dramatic happened on that crossing – it was one of many westbound transits of Puget Sound.

Facing page: With the winter Sun low in the southern sky and diffused by a broken layer of clouds, the skyline facing towards the southwest is bathed in a wash of soft light.

Below: A fast foot ferry, on loan to the WSF system and so not the usual WSF green, crosses satin-smooth water in Elliott Bay as it approaches Alki Point heading southwest.

These pages: Where the incoming tide meets the standing waters of low tide, a "tideline" is formed, plainly visible on the surface of the Sound.

Following pages, overleaf: Moments before the outbound ferry crossed the tideline shown in the pictures on these pages, the Tacoma – *inbound from Bainbridge – crossed that line on her journey east.*

At right: Rays of sunlight splash down onto the Sound through the narrow slits between parallel courses of clouds.

Below: In the distance, the ferry from Bainbridge nears Seattle as the city's towers fade into the waning of the day.

Following pages, overleaf: A ferry inbound for Seattle from Bremerton voyages eastward leaving the sunset behind.

As the Sun sets, its last rays reach under the clouds to brush the water and the city with the day's final gleaming.

Broken clouds and oblique late-day light paint above the Sound, and the water, with its many varied surfaces, reinterprets that display from below.

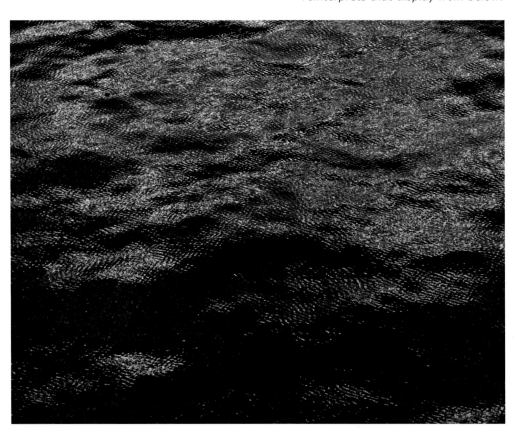

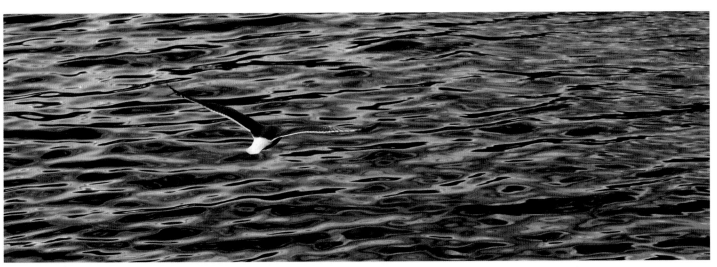

Deck crew members move to their docking positions as the ferry nears its slip; the car ramp and passenger gangway are lowered; and the outpouring of passengers begins. The 4:40 p.m. and 5:30 p.m. weekday sailings from Seattle are the busiest westbound commuter trips.

For several thousand people who live west of Seattle
but work in that city, ferries are how we commute.
We learn the rhythms of the transit system,
the scheduled sailings, walkways, ramps.
The passage becomes a daily ritual.

A ferry crosses the Sound, carrying commuters home.
The journey lasts about an hour, from end to end.

Nothing extraordinary or dramatic happens on this
particular crossing of the water, or on most crossings –
there are many such transits of Puget Sound.

The ferries ceaselessly crisscross the Sound.

As one crossing begins, another has ended.

It is impossible to anticipate exactly what any one crossing will bring, but it is almost certain that no two crossings are ever precisely alike.

Take a ride on a ferry. The mountains, skies, and sea are out there. When they smile at one another, good fortune can present a memorable passage. There will never be another crossing quite like the one that awaits you.

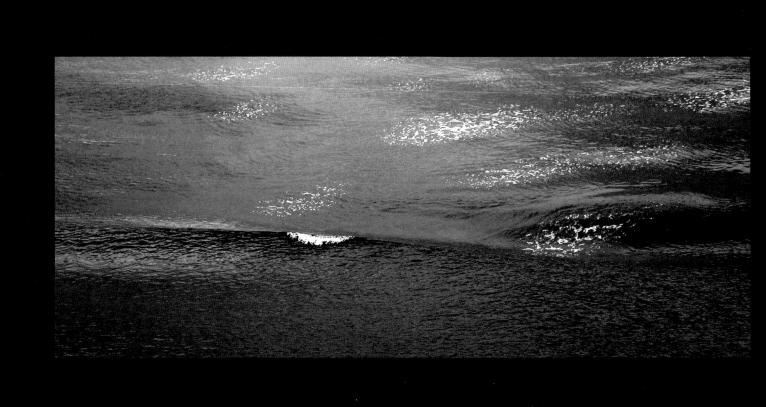

Addenda:

Facts for those who like to collect them:

° Ferry terminals have to accommodate the complete tidal range of Puget Sound. The various decks of a ferry retain consistent distances above the surface of the water (minor loading effects aside), but the level of the water itself rises and falls with the tides. At Seattle, the average difference between the peaks of high tides and low tides is about 12 feet, but periodic extreme high and low tides produce variations of as much as 18 feet. (The unusual extremes are roughly +14' to -4'.) This means that the water-side ends of all vehicle ramps and foot-passenger gangways and passageways must be flexible enough to drop or rise to meet the level of a ferry in its slip. Vehicle and foot passenger ramps can be raised and lowered at their outer (water-side) ends to match the level of the ferry's deck. The tunnels for walk-ons are like the boarding ramps in use at airports – both resemble elongated pieces of square tubing. Because the ends of the ramps at the slips must be able to move vertically to follow changes of deck height driven by the tidal range, the final segments of these ramps are long enough (about 80 to 90 feet)

The Kitsap, *inbound from Bremerton near sunset, passes north of Harbor Island.*

so that, even when the outer end is raised or lowered, the ramps will provide passengers and vehicles with a reasonable grade (one that is not too steep). They also are equipped with heavy counter-weights to allow moving them more easily.

○ According to WSF, the average number of one-way transits of the Sound each day on the Seattle/Bainbridge route is 17,500. There are 23 sailings from each of these terminals on weekdays, for 46 crossings. If the passenger traffic followed an "average", then each ferry would carry about 400 people (about one-sixth of the capacity of the largest boats). Passenger loads are actually very "lumpy" – some boats are filled to capacity while others sail almost empty. Having regular service available, however, is viewed as important to ensure that commuters and others who need to cross the Sound will not face having too few and mostly overcrowded boats.

○ The effects of disrupted ferry service were demonstrated in the 1948 Black Ball Line "ferry strike", when Captain Alexander Peabody (who owned most docking facilities and boats) tied up his boats for nine days after being denied a 30% fare increase. Alternative transit efforts cobbled together with other boats and land transport did not succeed, and the area suffered significantly. This experience helped motivate the State to acquire most of the Black Ball Line in 1951.

○ In the maritime world, a "collision" occurs when two moving ships or barges (or other objects in motion) run into each other. If a moving ship instead strikes a stationary object, the term "allision" applies. Ferries experience few collisions, but far more often suffer an allision – running into objects such as a breakwater, pier, or dock. A photographic history of the ferry system and of some of the several ferry and dock allisions is shown on the sloped walkway between the main level of the Seattle ferry terminal and the sidewalk along the west side

of Alaskan Way. The Colman Dock (at the Seattle terminal) has been hit on multiple occasions, and the clock that is now mounted on the east side of the terminal once ended up floating in Elliott Bay. Studying the history of those events during a slow walk up or down the terminal ramp might discourage the timid from taking a "front of the boat" position.

○ Ships can leave behind another form of "track" – a cloud trail created when moisture condenses on or around very small fuel exhaust particles. Satellite photos can show plumes extending hundreds of miles behind cargo ships, particularly at sea, where they customarily burn low-grade (almost tarry) "bunker fuel". When cargo ships approach coastal areas and harbors, they typically shift over to cleaner but more expensive fuels.

○ The larger ferries burn diesel fuel to generate electricity; the propellers are driven not directly by a combustion engine, but indirectly through power delivered to large electric motors located at each end of the boat. The front and rear props thus can be operated independently, both driving the boat in the same direction or with their thrusts countering each other (for more delicate maneuvering). During parts of 2006 and 2007, passengers with a particularly acute sense for odors may have wondered whether the exhaust from the ferries' diesel-electric engines smelled a little strange. If so, it may have been because of a then-ongoing experiment with using bio-diesel formulated with used grease from deep-fat fryers; in practice, however, the fuel (or residual food fragments) reportedly fouled the fuel systems and engines of the ferries. In 2008, WSF announced plans to repeat the experiment, with the expectation that newer techniques for refining bio-diesel would produce a fuel that will function better.

○ [This space is reserved for that one vital but missing fact.]

About the author

Michael Diehl started commuting to Seattle by ferry in August 2005.

That experience quickly led to using a camera during those voyages. The varied scenery and light presented by the Sound provided fresh reasons each day for continuing the custom. No day repeated another.

Crossings began as an Internet posting with about 50 pages of text and photographs, created and placed on the Web as a way to show friends and relatives what it was like to ride the ferries. As the website was referred on to others and comments began to flow in, the idea grew of developing the concept into a more complete photographic essay.

Photograph by Judith Rogerson

Acknowledgements

Two individuals whose gifts to this project were particularly significant are now beyond receiving any personal thanks – Gilbert Barrera of San Antonio, who took on and taught a completely unskilled apprentice photojournalist in 1968, and David Marshall, who ten years later in Berkeley provided a setting that allowed combining photography, writing and design for dozens of publications.

Several people were kind enough to review and comment on pre-publication draft mockups of *Crossings*. They are, in no particular sequence: Judith, whose frank responses to photographs, text and page designs were always illuminating; Roger Cunnane, a former merchant ship captain whose retirement life includes frequent cross-Sound ferry journeys, and John Kimmerlein, a daily Bainbridge-to-Seattle ferry commuter and former skipper who now is a specialist in admiralty law, both of whom scrutinized sections describing matters familiar to experienced sea-goers; Christi Lockhart, another sometime photographer who likewise toils primarily in other, drier vineyards; Tom Twigg, a fellow kayaker and ferry commuter, and a photographer and Internet publication production designer; and Emmanuelle Donaldson, a member of the WSF system's deck crew, who was asked to ensure that *Crossings* was consistently truthful.

A book list (a few pertinent books of possible interest):

Nonfiction

° *Olympic: A Visitor's Companion*, George Weurther (the geologic, human and natural history of the Olympic Peninsula)

° *Passage to Juneau: A Sea and Its Meanings*, Jonathan Raban (a sailing trip from Seattle is the theme for multiple levels of narrative, including the relationships of Native Peoples and newcomers to the land and sea)

° *Rare Earth: Why Complex Life Is Uncommon in the Universe*, Peter Ward & Donald Brownlee (a study of the many and complex forces that support higher forms of life on Earth, and a celebration of how extraordinary and delicate their balance must be for life-sustaining conditions)

° *Island in the Sound*, Hazel Heckman (an unadorned description of life on a small island in the South Sound, where ferry service is the only connection to the mainland)

° *Our Changing Planet: The View from Space*, Michael King et al. (depictions of Earth based on long-term observations, including comparing many years of satellite photographs)

° *The Final Forest: The Battle for the Last Great Trees of the Pacific Northwest*, William Dietrich (a now somewhat dated but very comprehensive and balanced look at the role, history and practices of logging and forestry in the region)

° *Wintergreen: Rambles in a Ravaged Land*, Robert Michael Pyle (a naturalist's low-key description of the geography, landscapes, flora and fauna of the heavily logged Willapa Hills south of the base of the Olympic Peninsula)

Relevant history

° *Vancouver's Voyage: Charting the Northwest Coast*, Robin Fisher (a portrayal of Captain George Vancouver's four-year mapping of some 1,000 miles of previously uncharted coasts)

° *The Ferries of Puget Sound (Images of America)*, Steven Pickens (a retrospective about the history of ferries on the Sound with more than 200 photographs)

° *Puget Sound Ferries: From Canoe to Catamaran*, Carolyn Neal & Thomas Janus (history and anecdotes about ferries on the Sound)

Informative fiction about the region

° *Alaska*, James Michener (Section X, a clear and fascinating account of the life cycle of salmon in the northern Pacific)

° *The Living*, Annie Dillard (the lives of early settlers in the Northwest)

° *Snow Falling on Cedars*, David Guterson (a story of life and a mystery on a fictional Puget Sound island from which Americans of Japanese ancestry were taken for internment during World War II)

An illustrated guide to ferry jargon: "picklefork" – "jackstaff" – "car tunnel"

The rounded nose of the ferry close to the water is where the car-loading ramp rests, allowing vehicles to drive on and off the ferry. To accommodate tall loads moving into or out of the car tunnel on a ramp (which can be steep in low-tide periods), the center portion of the main deck (one level higher) is cut away.

The cutout in the main deck at each end of the boat creates two projections around the cutout area described as a "picklefork". The railings on these projections include a movable segment for foot passenger loading. A "jackstaff", traditionally used for flags, extends out above the main deck at each end of the boat.

This page, above: A picklefork and the nose of the ferry where vehicles load, viewed from above.

Facing page, at right: A jackstaff, the cutaway portion of the main deck directly over the car tunnel entrance, and the resulting picklefork, viewed from the walkway around the outside of the upper deck.

Facing page, at far right: The underside of the picklefork from the car deck (upper photograph) and the interior of the car deck showing a ramp used for loading autos onto the outside upper car tier.

Ferry jargon:
"dolphins" – "wingwalls"

Ferries are stabilized in slips for loading and unloading by using the propeller and rudder located at the seaward end to keep the boat's land-side end pressed against structures of pilings that cradle the boat's nose ("wingwalls") as well as large fenders alongside the boat ("dolphins").

The photograph at left shows a view looking towards the slip and along the outer deck railing of a ferry taking on passengers in Eagle Harbor. The ferry's side is pressed against a dolphin (the structure in the foreground with the orange and white triangular marker), while the boat's prow is cradled between the wingwalls.

Paired wingwalls in a slip at the Seattle terminal are shown in the photograph at right, and a floating concrete dolphin from the same location is shown below. Unlike the floating, moored dolphins in Seattle, those around Bainbridge's terminal are affixed to the harbor bottom.

Ferry jargon: "Pier 52" – "Colman Dock" – "Colman Clock"

Piers on Seattle's waterfront are numbered (the numbers increase moving from south to north, but gaps exist in the sequence). The main WSF terminal building is located at Pier 52, which was historically known as the Colman Dock.

In the late 1800s, a clock was placed at the west end of that dock, atop a wooden tower. A ship hit the dock, and the clock tumbled into Elliott Bay. Rescued, it then was forgotten until it was found, restored, and placed outside the terminal.